# THERE ARE NO HOSPITALS IN RUSSIA

*A Memoir*

Santino DeFranco

Copyright © 2022 by Santino DeFranco

All rights reserved. No part of this publication may be reproduced, distributed, or transmitted in any form or by any means, including photocopying, recording, or other electronic or mechanical methods, without the prior written permission of the publisher, except in the case of brief quotations embodied in critical reviews and certain other noncommercial uses permitted by copyright law. For permission requests, write to the publisher, addressed "Attention: Permissions Coordinator," at the address below.

Golden Fleece Press
PO Box 1464,
Centreville, VA 20122
www.goldenfleecepress.com

Special discounts are available on quantity purchases by corporations, associations, and others. For details, contact the publisher at the address above.

Kindle ISBN 13: 978-1-942195-73-3
Print ISBN 13: 978-1-942195-70-2
Pdf ISBN 13: 978-1-942195-71-9

Printed in the United States of America
First Edition
        10 9 8 7 6 5 4 3 2 1

# DEDICATION

*I'd like to dedicate this book to my wife, Kindal. She's an oak, and none of this would have been possible without her.*

# 1

**May 2005:**

My hands trembled as I flipped my cell phone shut. I circled my kitchen back and forth in confusion. While pacing, I noticed my clammy hands. *Was that a sign? Is that something?* When I looked down at my palms, the sight of the callouses just below my fingers brought me back to reality. *Phew. I just worked out. That's right. The sweat's from the workout.* I felt like a drunk bird, unable to think clearly as I pegged my legs down the hallway to my bathroom. I tore my clothes off and turned the shower knob and stared at the hot water spraying. I didn't want to go to the hospital smelling like an old gym sock, but the water frightened me. *What if I go unconscious and fall? What if the aneurysm pops or whatever the hell they do? What If I drown in the shower before Steve gets here? Fuck it.* I jumped in and spastically ran my fingers through my hair and across my body with a lather of soap. Once my body was free of the sudsy foam, I wrapped my arms around my chest, gripping my shoulders, and slunk to the bottom of the tub. As my body lurched by the heaves of a crying fit, my tears mixed with the water of the shower and vanished down the drain, never to have a life of their own.

\*\*\*

As it turns out, I'd always thought I was destined for greatness. I don't know if that stemmed from my own megalomania and naive narcissism, or from the dream world I lived in and the superheroes I wished I could be like as a kid. So, when Dana White, the president of the UFC, called me after I had auditioned for *The Ultimate Fighter,* a reality TV show that put 16 grown men in a house to live together and beat each other up in hopes of attaining a contract with the Ultimate Fighting Championships (UFC), I beamed with confidence. I knew I had made it in life.

Seeing the head of the UFC on my caller ID in May of 2005, could have only meant one thing: good news. If I hadn't made it into the house, I would have gotten a form letter. Or one of the producers or assistants would have informed me that I didn't make the cut. Nope. This was the man himself. This meant my shit life, my shit upbringing, my shit future had changed for the better. This meant I was flying to Vegas in a couple of days to start the first day of my journey toward greatness. To superstardom.

\* \* \*

Upon exiting the plane, heading for my audition for the second season of *The Ultimate Fighter*, I felt as if I were somehow transported to a top-secret spy mission by the way the handlers were treating it. First, there was a person waiting for me at baggage claim, but he didn't have my name on a piece of cardboard or anything normal. He had the number "46" written down—the number I was given as my "identification" for when I arrived. Me, giddy with excitement and being the chatty mouse I am, was trying to spark up a conversation with my new friend.

"Hey, man. What's up? I'm glad to be off that plane," I said.

"Follow me please," he replied. *Not talkative I see.*

Then, I noticed the earpiece and he started talking into his sleeve like a secret service agent.

"I have number 46 here. We're heading out of baggage claim."

*Seriously?*

We continued to walk out the door, until he put his arm up as if we were stopping short in a *Seinfeld* episode, and he said into his sleeve, "We're at the door."

Then he turned to me and said, "We have to wait here for a minute, 'til the others pass. They don't want any of you seeing each other."

*What? Are we on our way to fucking Thunder Dome or something?*

That type of weirdness continued until we got to the hotel, one of the Station Casinos. My handler would talk into his sleeve, and we either continued or waited, which was becoming increasingly annoying—but what the hell did I have going on? He then opened my door and I walked in.

"Here's your room. You can't leave at all, so you aren't getting a room key," said the secret agent.

"What about food?"

"Everything will be brought to your room. Someone will be up in a bit to give you a menu and go over all the details with you."

"So, I can't leave here at all? Can I open the door?" I asked.

"No."

"Can I crack the door just a sliver and peek out?" I joked.

"No. If you leave the room for any reason, you will immediately be put on a plane back home and be disqualified for consideration for the show. And, I need to take your cell phone. No calls either."

"Very well, then."

"Good luck," he said and left me in my room alone.

Just as my secret agent friend said, someone was at my door within the hour to go over everything with me and take me to my first interview. She told me I was going to go have a short interview with two producers on camera to see how comfortable I seemed in front of an audience, and more importantly, the camera. She also gave me a menu card that I ordered my dinner and breakfast from. I ordered the chicken with a side of rice and broccoli.

There was more stop and go traveling to get to the interview room to ensure potential contestants remained unknown to one another. I was kind of glad I had a few more minutes to prepare myself mentally. I knew the producers, and the UFC, were looking more for characters than fighters. Of course, if the characters could fight, better, but their main goal was TV ratings, and I knew that.

When I walked into the hotel room-turned-TV-studio there were two producers waiting for me: a man and a woman. They sat me down and began asking me questions in front of a camera that had cords and wires running into the adjacent room.

They started with all the usual stuff. Where was I from? Why did I think I was a good fit for the show? I gave them my most obnoxious answers. "What does it matter where I'm from? It only matters where I'm going. I'm the best in the world and I'll beat anyone in front of me." And so on. Then, I started questioning the questioners.

"I actually have a question for you. Did you work on the last season of the show?"

"He did, but this is my first time working on the show," the woman said.

"Then, you! Are you responsible for putting Jason Thacker on the show? That's what I want to know."

"Not really. We don't get the final say in who goes on or not," the man said laughing hysterically.

"I want to know who the hell was responsible for that? That guy had never fought in his life. Who can get fired for that? We need to find that out. Somebody needs to be fired for that one." I continued my rant for many minutes until we were all thoroughly laughed out and the interview concluded. As I was standing up to walk out, Dana White came in from the adjacent room and looked at me.

"I'm the asshole responsible for putting Jason Thacker on the show," he said to me.

"What the hell were you thinking?" I demanded.

"Well, we need different types of personalities on the show. We need your good, nice kids like Thacker, and we need your foul mouthed, mother slapping assholes like yourself," he said with a smile on his face.

"Good point, but I would never hit my mother."

It worked. My obnoxiousness got me through to another interview, which consisted of me talking to a large table filled with TV executives, including Craig Piligian (the executive producer), and Dana White. After more of my nonsensical ramblings I knew I was a lock for the show.

"Dana, what the fuck are we going to do with this kid?" Piligian asked.

"I don't know, but I like him," Dana said.

"I mean, the people watching aren't going to get the full effect from their TV. I am physically dizzy from listening to him. I mean I am actually dizzy. I'm not even sure it's possible for that to travel over the airwaves."

I left with confidence and went back to my room where I was served my dinner. I took a bite of the chicken I'd ordered earlier and painfully swallowed the cardboard piece of meat. It was a broiled breast with no seasonings or sauces on it, served with steamed broccoli with no seasonings or sauces on it, accompanied by a side of rice with no seasonings or sauces on it. I ate the rice. Later that night I was told I would be staying for the medical tests. There were no tests the following day, Tuesday, but on Wednesday I would have my MRI and ophthalmologist exam.

When Wednesday came around, I finally saw the faces of the other contestants in the running when we were shuttled to the doctor's office. While waiting for tests, I talked with Nate Marquardt, a fighter that would go on to have a long, illustrious career with the UFC. He was big for a 185lb human, and would have been huge for welterweight, one of the weight classes featured during the second season. He told me he wasn't planning on becoming a contestant for the show, he knew he was too big, and didn't really want to be on the show anyway. He was there to open a dialogue with the UFC after a long stint in Japan fighting for Pancrase. I chatted up Keith Jardine for a while too. We were talking about literature, me talking of my love of Russian authors; him about being a Bukowski fan. Can't blame him for that.

The days were boring. The TV had limited channels. I was imprisoned in a casino and the casino wanted their guests to spend their time—and money—gambling, not in their rooms. I had the same variation of the same meal every dinner, regardless of what I ordered. If I ordered the chicken or salmon, it was the same unflavored rubbish. I did bring a book, *Crime and Punishment,* a massive block of text that I finished during my time in solitude, in between my jumping on the bed and acting like a three-year-old.

On my final day there I was grouped with Melvin Guillard, Joe Stevenson, Jason Von Flue, and others. We were off to have our urine analyzed for drugs: recreational and performance enhancing. Lumped in a room, unable to use the bathroom to ensure we could piss while a lab worker sat 10 inches from our dick to actually see the urine go from body to cup, we talked amongst each other. The talking quickly turned to agitation as Von Flue went in to offer his urine sample. He was in the room for over an hour leaving the rest of the bladders in the room swollen and uncomfortable. We yelled at him to come out and that he could go back in after the rest of us went. He didn't and we had to listen to Melvin Guillard tell us of his glories for as long as he had functioning ears around him.

"Man, I ain't never been submitted in an MMA fight. I don't care who it is, they're not getting me down to submit me. And, stand up? Oh, hell no. I'm undefeated in kick boxing matches. I've been to Japan and fought three times in shoot boxing and kick boxing matches and have won them all," Guillard boasted.

Nobody said a word. We were all too uncomfortable to put up with anything or even speak by the time Melvin started. Our bladders could handle no more. Then, Melvin stopped mid rant and turned to me.

"You look familiar. Where do I know you from?" he said to me.

"Really?" I asked. "We fought last November."

"Who won," Joe Stevenson asked.

I didn't say a word and turned to Melvin.

"Oh, he did. He choked me with a guillotine or something," Melvin said. It was actually a triangle choke.

The room laughed, and poked fun at his un-submittable tirade, but only momentarily, as the door to the bathroom finally opened and Von Flue exited.

"Finally, you're out. Asshole," someone said.

"I couldn't go," Von Flue said, dejected. "I couldn't go with him looking right at my dick. Creeped me out."

"Wait, so you still didn't piss?" I asked.

"No, I'll go in again after you guys go," he said.

After the rest of us had pissed in a small cup while someone watched, Von Flue went back in. Forty minutes later he came out victorious.

*　*　*

"Hey, Dana," I said as I saw his number on my caller ID a few days after the audition. "How's it going?" My excitement was palpable. He could probably feel part of my cheek on his own, as my face stretched so wide with my grin.

"Hey, kid, do you have health insurance?" Dana asked.

"No. But I can get some if I need to for the show. I can start looking now. Let me know the details of what I need and I can get it today."

"No. It's not like that," he said, and after a pause added, "Do you have family there?"

"Yeah, my father lives here."

"You need to call him and you need to go to the hospital right now."

"What? Why? What's wrong?"

"I—I don't even want to tell you. You need to go to the hospital, right now."

"Seriously, you have to tell me what the hell is going on."

"Man...okay. The doctors found two brain aneurysms during your MRI."

"What is that? What's a brain aneurysm?"

"I don't really know, kid, which is why you need to get to the doctor immediately. Sorry, kid."

And like that, my fighting career was over.

I called my friend and roommate, Steve, to come take me to the hospital. Then I called my girlfriend, Kindal, to deliver the news to her as well.

After Steve picked me up, after missing about thirty exits on the freeway correctly, we got to the hospital. I approached the counter to check in and informed the woman that I was just told I had a brain aneurysm and that I needed to see a doctor immediately.

"Fill this out, and sign in here. When you're done with the paper work, bring it back up here."

I looked at Steve quizzically. He reciprocated my confusion. We sat down in the waiting area.

"Well, they don't seem too concerned about it. So, that seems like a good thing, right? You're probably not gonna die right this minute. Like right here and now," he said, always the one for logic.

When I did see the doctor, he reiterated what Dana had told me—that I would never fight again—and also, until the brain aneurysm was corrected (entailing surgery), I couldn't increase my inter-cranial pressure at all. That meant no getting punched, wrestling or working out in any form.

"What about push-ups. You know, body weight exercises?" I asked.

"No. None at all. You could cause too much pressure to build up in your brain and the aneurysm could rupture. And, actually, if you need to go to the bathroom—have a bowel movement—you need to make sure you don't push too hard as that could rupture it too."

*Seriously? I can't take a forceful shit!?*

Fortunately, I wasn't at an immediate risk of death. The aneurysm, attached to my carotid artery, behind my left eye wasn't at risk of rupturing, and was relatively small. There was also just one aneurysm. Dana was incorrect in what he told me. The other "issue" was that I had an extra artery in my brain that connected two other major arteries—which really wasn't a big deal. All children are born with such an artery, but most disappear before adulthood. However, those extra arteries are seen more commonly in those with brain aneurysms, which, in case you're wondering, is a stretched out part of an artery that looks kind of like a balloon. The problem comes in when that balloon-shaped structure continues to expand, and just like a balloon, pops. The amount of pressure built up in the carotid artery would mean, if the aneurysm ruptured, that a massive amount of blood would go pouring into my brain and produce a massive stroke rendering me an invalid, or most likely, send me to my grave.

After the doctors gutted my dreams of fighting in the world's premier organization, I did what any self-pitying, woe-is-me, tantruming, 22-year-old would do: got shit-face drunk.

Kindal departed, leaving Steve and me to commiserate as a duo. We decided the best place to perform such an act would be at a dive hole-in-the-wall sushi restaurant near our house in Chandler, Arizona. We opted for the cold sake as opposed to the warm urine tasting drink that comes standard with a bomber, and, in between nostalgic reminiscing of great moments throughout my young career as a fighter and pontificating on our existential human condition, Steve would encourage me with positive glimpses of my future—none of which sounded as enticing as the could-have-would-haves of my life just hours earlier. As our speech slurred on, and our balance and perception waned, we thought the best course of action, considering our state, was to drive ourselves home. And with Steve behind the helm of his Jeep Rubicon, we proceeded to drive toward our home—though a detour up a tilting tree and into a concrete wall stopped our journey short.

The Jeep was smashed. There was no salvaging that beast. Running around like enraged penguins, Steve and I paced back and forth under the dark of night until a woman pulled up next to us. She barely cracked her window—she seemed a clever lady to keep us at such a distance considering our behavior.

Steve ran up to her window, smearing his own blood on it.

"Hey, can you give us a ride? Or, like, call someone for us. We've had a bit of an accident over here." He then walked away from her before she could answer and waved his hands in the air as he looked at his wrecked Jeep.

"I can't believe this!" Steve cried out.

While Steve looked surprised at the situation every time the destroyed Jeep that rested almost vertically in a tree came into his view, I ran around, stopping only to regularly grab my shins that were scraped and in pain due to me lifting my legs immediately prior to impact—and hitting the passenger "oh shit" bar that lay horizontally above the glove box.

A few minutes later the police showed up. The Jeep was towed. Steve was taken in for driving while intoxicated, and I was arrested for an old warrant for urinating in public. The day had definitely begun better than it ended.

Kindal was smart to leave the two of us to our own debauched version of a pity-party.

\* \* \*

Nine months earlier, I was disenchanted with my present MMA training situation, and so I decided to sublease some space from a Kung Fu instructor, Sifu Gonzalez, and train people myself, in hopes of building a gym of my own. Gonzalez was a long-haired Mexican man who had the cheesy, fake mystique most traditional martial arts instructors evoke. It's as though they need to convince others of some supernatural power in order to attract students. Gonzales was no different, and his only two students I ever saw train with him seemed equally as "mystical." Somehow, throughout my short tenure of running my own Brazilian Jiu Jitsu school, a Marine recruiter, Justin, started training with me in hopes of taking the first steps to a long and illustrious career. He was an arrogant fellow (as I said, he was a Marine), but a good enough human. Time and again, Justin would invite me out with him and his girlfriend to clubs and restaurants and bars, to which I would always decline, until one day, for whatever reason, I acquiesced.

At a large table on the patio of a North Scottsdale (one of the more affluent areas of Phoenix) restaurant/bar, I was introduced to Justin's girlfriend, Katie, and her friend, Jill, the birthday girl and the reason for the outing. Across from me sat Kindal, a lovely creature with blonde streaks in her hair and bangs that fell to her green eyes. She was quiet at first, but eventually she opened up into conversation with me, although we were constantly being interrupted by another of the girls that was making all attempts to block us from talking. I think she had already planned her evening out with me, and Kindal was nowhere in those plans. Through the annoyances, though, I threw every trick, joke, and charm I could muster up at Kindal in hopes of convincing her to give me the time of day—even going as far as lying about my age. See, she was from a well-to-do family of dentists, doctors, lawyers, and other productive members of society—and she was 26 years old. I came from a line of insanity, depression, and disability—and, was 22 years old at the time. I knew there was no way in hell that this woman—this gorgeous, functioning member of society—was going to date a vagabond fighter who was four years younger than her. So, I told her I was 25 years old.

"But, what about the fighting? I don't like fighting," Kindal said.

"I do that as a job. A profession. I never get into street fights, and I don't get into trouble. I'm not like that at all. Honestly, I grew up wrestling and boxing, and started training and fighting after I was done wrestling. Seriously, I haven't been in a street fight since I was a freshman in high school or something around that time."

This type of uneasiness continued intermittently as we flirted and laughed for hours. Finally, when the time came to leave, her defenses were lowered enough to give me her phone number and agree to get together at a later time. She left the bar and Justin walked Katie to her car while I waited in the parking lot in his Mitsubishi Eclipse.

Tending to my impatience, I turned and twisted my head in hopes of seeing Justin come to the rescue—I'd been sitting in the car for nearly fifteen minutes. No such luck, though I did see a group of five or six people running around in the parking lot. After a few skips and turns, one ran between Justin's car (on the passenger side, where I was sitting) and the car next to it. A moment later two other people ran by, banging their hands on the car's roof, just above my head. Annoyed at the situation, and for my own safety, I opened the car door and stood in between the door and the car, but I didn't make direct eye contact. I was tired and didn't want to provoke anyone, especially if they were just running around drunk and having a good time.

From behind me came a voice, and I saw a flash of a camera.

"Now I know who the fuck you are, bitch! You try to anything, or try to run, I know who the fuck you are. I got your license plate now, bitch!"

*Oh shit! Someone's about to get in a lot of trouble!* I thought, then turned around and looked for the recipient of the verbal assault. Then I looked around and only found myself in the parking lot besides the group of miscreants with the yeller.

"Oh, me? Naw, man, you must think I'm someone else. I'm just waiting for my friend so we can go home."

"Fuck you, man! You try anything, I know who you are!"

The yeller continued his tirade for another minute, which must have been loud enough for Justin to hear from where he was standing, as he and Katie came back from the road.

"Everything okay over here, guys?" Justin asked.

"Fuck you! And fuck your bitch! You hear that, bitch? Fuck you!"

At this point, I walked toward Justin and Katie and assured Justin we should just leave the crazies to themselves and be on our way. When I turned to walk toward Justin's car, the yeller sucker-punched me in the jaw, whipping my head to the side. Even after the punch, though, for whatever reason, I was still calm and didn't want to fight with a group of seemingly drugged up nuts in a random parking lot.

"No, don't worry about it," I said to Justin. "Let's just get the hell outta here. I'm fine."

As I turned again toward Justin's car, the remainder of the group surrounded us like a 1980's kung fu movie, preventing an unobstructed escape.

"What the hell's wrong with you? All I want to do is go home and go to bed. Are you retarded or something?" I said to the angry yeller.

The guy came at me and swung a wild haymaker. I barely acknowledged it and stepped in close to him jamming his punch. I then threw him to the ground and choked him. As I was squeezing his neck, he tapped my arm to indicate that he was "done with the fight," which I thought was weird, as this was long before MMA or submission fighting was popular.

"This is a street fight. You can't tap out in a street fight."

He quickly began grunting and snoring. Once he went limp I let him go. As I stood up a wave of heat and annoyance and rage flooded my body. All I wanted to do was go home, but I couldn't because this unconscious asshole below me wouldn't allow for it. *He hit me when I wasn't looking,* I thought.

As my elbow made contact with his face, his head ricocheted off of the pavement. Again. And again.

One of his friends ran toward me and tried to kick me in the face, but Justin pushed him aside.

I stood up.

"You guys are all assholes," I said. "All I wanted to do was go home and go to bed. Who's next. Who else wants to end up like him," I said and pointed to the motionless body that lay on the ground.

The rest of the crew decided that they did not, indeed, want to end up like their friend on the ground, who was starting to wake up as we left. As we drove off, I saw him standing in the sideview mirror.

I went home with a sore jaw, and called Kindal a few days later.

"So, I'd like to really go out with you, but I don't think I can for a few weeks. I kind of broke my jaw and it's wired shut."

"Yeah, Katie told me you got in a fight right after I left."

"I know it sounds crazy, but that never—"

"Don't worry. She told me it wasn't your fault and that you tried everything not to fight. She actually said it was pretty cool."

\* \* \*

I was no longer a fighter and I felt lost. Empty. There was a void. What could it be filled with? I'd only had a plan "A" and the doctors had just informed me that I'd need to formulate a plan "B". I'd known my entire adult life that I was going to be a professional fighter. I trained two, four, sometimes six hours a day in a sweaty little gym in Arizona. I was beyond a nine-to-five. That was for the people that weren't special like me. The chip on my shoulder was too big; my head was too big. My naivety was grand, and I could hardly imagine me as being one of "those people" that finds a job and climbs the corporate ladder.

I'd read too much Russian literature and thought like Raskolnikov—I *thought* I was above the rest. I *thought* I was special. However, I *knew* if I didn't get a job immediately, I'd unravel into a pitiful, pathetic human, always feeling sorry for himself. With haste, I searched for jobs. I figured I could have a grand, big ol' pity party after I had something set up.

After I had some way to make a living. After I had something to keep me in the graces of Kindal. I knew she didn't love me for money. I didn't really have any when we met or throughout our relationship; she'd love me as a pauper. But she deserved better than that. And I would be damned if I was going to let her love a loser—let her love someone who didn't love her enough to pick himself up and find a way in life.

No, I wasn't special, and, on top of it, I was scared. *What does someone like me do for a job?* I didn't have any work experience outside of a part-time job working for Circuit City, selling electronics. I didn't have any education outside of a few community college credits. I didn't know anything about anything outside of fighting, so I really was at a loss for how I was going to break into the job market. I was like so many retired boxers and fighters before me, who lived their entire lives without a second thought of "what happens after I'm done." And like so many of them, when it was all said and done, I had nothing. Would I wind up a laborer or dishwasher like so many before me? Like so many unnamed, tough guys with nothing to show but cauliflower ear and smashed noses and rigid hands.

A few days later I walked back into my old gym, Arizona Combat Sports, and talked with my trainer at the time, Trevor Lally. With me, I brought my bag of training gear: boxing gloves, shin pads, head gear.

I'd received a warm welcome, but that awkwardness was in the air. Just like when the loved one of a friend dies and you tell them it's okay and give your condolences, but nobody really knows what to say after that. What do you say when you know something's wrong, that it won't be okay—at least in the sense that we want it to be—and then have to see the widow or father or mother of someone who's died? What do you say when someone's dreams die? I'm not sure I know the answer to that. I'm not sure anyone knows the answer to that. I'm pretty sure nobody at that gym, at that time, knew the answer to that. And if they did, they certainly didn't say it to me. And I certainly didn't want to hear any condolences from anyone.

My career was dead.
My dream was dead.

I saw an old training partner, Truman, the man I credit my boxing skills to. After the "hellos" and "I'm so sorrys" from the room, I asked Truman, "I have this whole bag of gear. You want it? It'll just sit at my place unused."

He turned his head away from me for a minute and avoided eye contact as he shook his head in the negative.

"It's not right. I can't do that. You hang on to that stuff. It's too weird, Santino. Too weird."

I understood what he was saying, and it surely was too weird. I left it at that and talked with Trevor, who was also the owner of the gym. He told me I could use the gym as work experience. I could write down that I had sales and marketing and promotions experience. Whatever I needed and however I needed to write it was okay with him. Carte blanche to build my resume. He just told me to make sure I call him before an employer called, so he knew what to tell them.

That saved me, right there. It lifted me. I had a new start. It was small, but it was something. I wasn't a dishwasher yet.

# 2

**August 2000:**
 I was absolutely unprepared. I should not have been in that cage waiting for my opponent to enter so we could exchange punches and strangle holds in an enclosed chain-link fence. I should not have been in front of the raucous crowd that emitted thick, grey clouds of smoke forming curls into the air as it rose to the ceiling, never really dissipating, just gathering strength and density. And I sure as hell shouldn't have been wearing a striped Speedo, regardless of the situation, but especially with the ghostly pale and skinny limbs that were my own.
 Yet, there I stood: naive and scared and pale and cold, waiting in front of the crowd—waiting for...I don't know what. I was so unprepared I didn't even really know what I was expecting, or what I should have been expecting. I didn't know what I should have felt, and I had no idea my excitement would be equally accompanied by my fear. I didn't know that I wouldn't be able to eat the entire day, or that I'd need to piss every five minutes for hours leading up to the fight. I do know that when the MC announced over the crackling loudspeaker, "These are two of the best lightweights in the country," my heart fluttered, and the butterflies in my gut acted more like bees buzzing about, injecting me with their toxic stings. I thought, "Oh shit, this guy must be good, 'cause that's not me he's talking about."
 As I paced back and forth in my corner—which, in an octagonal cage, really equates to my half of the cage versus his half of the cage—I realized how cold I was getting. Moments prior, when I approached the cage and took my sweatshirt and sweatpants off, I was glazed in a warm, salty sweat. My muscles were ready to move. They would need to move quickly and flawlessly if I was going to leave with all of my teeth, or at least, my pride.

But, after pacing a few times in the cage, a cold front came over me. My fingertips were frozen and it felt like a cool breeze was blowing over my shoulders. I looked around to see if the air conditioning vent was above me. It wasn't. I was exposed to the air. I was exposed to the crowd and the reality of what was about to occur.

And it was cold.

Before I entered that cage I was clothed and protected by the world outside -- protected by laws and norms and sanity. Inside there was just me and another man locked in a cage as we punched and kicked and strangled each other for the pleasure of the voyeurs.

For the pleasure of our own sadism.

For the pleasure of our own egos as we try to fill some void somewhere within us that forces us to push beyond the boundaries of safe.

Through the veil of darkness, I saw the patrons waiting for the bloodshed. Most of the men in the bar wore cowboy hats; their bulbous bellies accompanied by either goatees or long beards. There were women with halter-tops and fake breasts, looking like they'd taken a break during their shift at the next-door strip club. Much more worrisome than the strippers were the older women with sagging breasts, like bowling balls had been placed in tube socks and hung from their chest. Their faces as smooth as gravel under a sheet, and their gossamer hair streaked with dye that couldn't fool Helen Keller. They yelled at the cage, as if in a bingo hall with their raspy voices.

Most hands, male and female, had fingers tightly pinched around cigarettes. And, of course, there was beer or whiskey in front of every onlooker. I spotted my girlfriend, Beth, and my father, leaning with their backs against a wall in the back of the room.

"And, in the blue corner," the MC announced. I had a hard time listening to the name he called out. It just sounded like the "waa waa waa" from the parents in a Charlie Brown cartoon. The only light in the bar was pointed directly at me, illuminating the cage. After my eyes broke focus from my father and everything else flew at me like I had vertigo. I saw the cage-side workers, the promoter of the event, the MC, random hands and cigarettes and booze-filled tables in the crowd. Everything swirled around me making me dizzy; then I saw someone approaching the cage door.

I may have not been ready, but I was excited.

\* \* \*

My father moved to California, then Arizona, while I finished senior year in high school in South Carolina. He said that since we fought every day, all day, it would be best for him to move away from me in order to keep our relationship strong. In reality, he just wanted to move again and didn't want to wait for me to finish high school. I don't think he wanted to deal with me, or my uncanny ability to be as self-absorbed as I was, either. He had, had it. I was about to graduate and would no longer be his problem. He said he would pay the rent, utilities, and send me money for food until my graduation, which was about four months away. Then he drove west.

My older sister, Adrianna, was still living with me and we were happy with the arrangement. The first 30 days were filled with booze, pot, and parties in between beach excursions. Somehow, I even managed to finish most of the schoolwork to graduate from high school. The fun was short lived, though. It was somewhere in the second month that we had a late notice tacked to our door telling us we had not paid rent. We thought, "there must be some mistake, right?"

"Dad," I heard Adrianna say into the phone, and I listened to the one side of the conversation I was able to.

"We just got a notice on the door that said rent was late."

"What?"

"What do you mean?"

"Well, what the hell are we supposed to do? What is Tino supposed to do? You do realize he's still in high school, right?"

"Goddammit! That's just great. Nice parenting job. It doesn't matter what you say. It doesn't matter. Bye."

She hung up the phone and looked at me, and groaned.

"He's not paying rent anymore," she said.

"What? What the hell do you mean?"

"He's not paying the goddamn rent anymore. He says he can't afford to. So, he's not going to pay it. He's not paying for anything."

"What the fuck is wrong with him? What are we going to do?" I asked.

"We have to pay it somehow."

And somehow, we did. Barely.

I worked the three to eleven shift at a hotel as a front desk agent. Adrianna worked at Circuit City. Our pennies were scarce, so I ate the frozen microwavable sandwiches and waffles meant for the continental breakfast the days I worked at the hotel. I shoved my pockets with as much as I could take home. We made just enough to keep from being evicted for a few months, and then decided it was more than we could handle.

We attended our oldest sister Chea's wedding, in Upstate New York, and said our goodbyes. I moved to Long Island with one of my father's old Vietnam buddies, Greg. I worked odd jobs for him, while I waited to begin courses at Wagner College, a private liberal arts school in Staten Island, where I planned to wrestle. Adrianna moved to Atlanta shortly after the wedding, and she lived with a friend and her parents.

Life worked out well for a few months while living with Greg. I painted a house on Lido Beach during the days and read Jack Kerouac books at night when I wasn't taking the train into the city to see my friend, Hallie, whom I dated off and on—in a long-distance sort of way—for years.

It was during my time in Long Island -- free to roam the enchanting streets of New York City, while drunk on life and sometimes alcohol or drugs -- that I started to pontificate on the existentialism of my existence. In between *Dharma Bums* and *Big Sur,* clarity focused in my brain like when the optometrist finally gets the exact prescription in front of your eyes. I started to think that I needed to make a name for myself somehow. I needed people to know who I was, and I needed people to remember my name long after I died. In my head I was going to follow Rudy Giuliani's path, and get into law. I'd prosecute big-time criminals, making a name for myself, and then enter politics. My undergraduate degree was going to be political science, then law school, then the world. The perfect plan. It'd be easy.

In a move of total ignorance and arrogance, I thought I would somehow be able to pay for my education at an expensive private college in Staten Island, NY. Even after I received a half academic scholarship (how I got it is still beyond me) I was short $20,000. I expected to receive some money for wrestling, too, but I didn't fill out my NCAA clearinghouse on time and wrestling money was not an option for the semester. The athletic department wasn't going to offer me money or help me out without multiple state championships under my belt. When the time for tuition came, I was unable to procure the funds and was dropped from my classes. My only thought was to seek the comfort of my father's roof, which I knew was close to Arizona State University. They had a spectacular wrestling team.

Within a couple of days, I was on a Greyhound bus to Charleston, South Carolina, to pick up my high school girlfriend, Beth. I'm still unclear why I called her and asked her to move to Scottsdale, Arizona, with me. I had hooked up with quite a few girls in New York during my time away from Beth, but I didn't ask any of them to come with me. I'm sure I still cared for Beth, but I think it had more to do with the fear of the unknown and of being alone. I also needed a buffer between my father and me. I was scared. Scared of the unknown. I didn't want to take that journey alone. Beth was deeply in love with me.

I met Beth while working as a waiter in South Carolina. She left her number on a piece of paper for me with a heart next to her name and hearts around the number. It was written in purple ink. She was a cute red-haired girl, with large breasts—exactly what seventeen-year-old boys hope for in a relationship.

When I called Beth from my room in Long Island to ask her if she wanted to accompany me to Arizona, she gave her answer immediately. I explained to her that we'd be living in my father's RV trailer. It didn't faze her. Her love was as strong as iron, and she'd be damned if something as trivial as wretched living conditions would get in the way of us. She was staying with her mother in North Carolina at the time, so we decided I would get to Charleston via Greyhound bus, then after staying with my sister for a few days, I'd borrow Adrianna's car (who was readying for her trip to Atlanta), and drive to Greenville to pick her up. She giddily acquiesced to my whimsical plans, and I arrived in South Carolina a few days later.

Beth was elated to see me, and I her. She was exactly as I'd remembered her, and her smile was as inviting as ever. A few days later, after visiting with her mother for a few days, Beth and I began our westward journey on a Greyhound.

On the bus, the smell of the bathroom next to our seats was strong enough to keep us disgusted, but just weak enough to keep us from vomiting. I looked around and was well aware that I was among the poor. All of us were sweaty uncomfortable and anxious to get to our destinations. Music blasted through headphones and late one night I heard a Mexican man yell out, "Policia! Policia!" And I thought we were trafficking illegals. Maybe we were. I wonder if he got to where he was going and if he still worries about the policia? We were traveling across the country like Sal and Dean and all the other beatniks. Only our driver wasn't racing a Jalopy through canyons and the back country of America in a speed induced frenzy, but rather taking his time, inching from one city to the next carrying a load of poor, disenchanted passengers.

The days on the bus were long and uncomfortable and somehow seemed even longer and more uncomfortable than they actually were. We sat in the back as much as possible where there was an extra seat that offered a scosche more room for our entangled legs. I was second-guessing everything. Should I have taken Beth? Should we be on our way to my Father's? What would we do? How would we live? Between my own insecurities and Beth's hand jobs, and greasy fast food, I nervously played out my Father's reaction to my traveling across the country to live with him again. I didn't know if we could stand being together, even for a short time, or if we'd immediately be at each other's throat. I didn't really care, though. At the time I didn't care what he said or did as long as it benefited me. I didn't even really wrap my head around the fact that he was even a real person.

I'm not sure I actually realized my father was a real person until years after his death. I always looked at him through the lens the selfish child does a parent, but never through the lens a person sees another person. He was always there—in our house, that is. Throughout all of the various towns and houses we lived in—and there were many—he and my sisters were the only constants in my tumultuous life. I don't know why we moved so much. My father was always running from something. He was running from creditors, from the ghosts in his head, from the dead babies in his nightmares. He was running from the wounds my mother inflicted on him when they divorced that never stopped bleeding, but constantly leaked blood out of him like a drizzle of honey dripping from a finger onto the floor before it could make its way into a child's mouth.

Even though he ran from the world, my father always took Chea, Adrianna, and me with him. Maybe he was running to protect us? Through all of the running and arguing I'm not sure I realized that he was even a real human like the rest of us that have cares and worries and dreams and the thought of any semblance of a life outside of raising my sisters, and me until much later. He was always just our father—that was it. He didn't date women after he and my mother got a divorce when I was five-years old. He didn't hang out with friends or socialize. He barely even worked during the course of my lifetime. He sat at our kitchen table chain-smoking cigarettes with his amber tinted fingertips, and ate copious amounts of medications—handfuls, multiple times a day. There were medications for his thyroid, heart, blood pressure, cholesterol, depression, anxiety, and eventually, muscle relaxers and painkillers. For years he just sat at the table, day in and day out, just being there. Present in body, not in mind.

Even though he'd never been in the running for the "Father Of The Year" award, my sisters and I always felt that where our father was, was where home was, which is why I was so disappointed to hear the nervousness in his voice when I called him from a Dallas bus station.

"Hello," he answered the phone.

"Hello there, Father," I said. I frequently called him Father or Pete.

"Oh hey, Tino, what are you up to? How's it going at Greg's?"

"Well, I'm not at Greg's anymore. I'm in Dallas, at a bus station. I'll be in Phoenix tomorrow." There was a silence on the phone, then I added, "Beth's with me."

"What?!" he cried. "Why are you coming here?"

"I don't have any other place to go. Can you pick us up?" I asked.

"Teen, I—I mean—I don't know if that's a good—Ya see, I just have my little trailer I'm in. The RV trailer."

"Oh, fine. I'll just stay here with Beth in this bus station until we figure things out. It's fine. Whatever. We'll be fine."

"Don't be like that, Tino. Ah hell. I guess—well, I guess you can stay with me," he said, his voice deflated. Defeated. "What's the address of the bus station, and what time do you get in?" He sighed heavily, and I knew it was not a ploy to make me feel bad. He was very worried about my arrival. Though he was terrified of my arrival, I also knew he wouldn't let me down. He would say "yes" and we would be together once again.

The next day when we pulled in to the Phoenix bus station the air looked hot. The shimmering heat blurred the outlines of cars and lampposts and buildings. Beth and I stepped off the bus and were welcomed with a slap in the face by an inferno that should not be inhabited. It's goddamn hot in Phoenix. I watched the weather forecast and saw the temperatures were in the triple digits. I never imagined it would be as assaulting as it was. Nobody can prepare for heat like that. It just comes and swarms around you, and permeates your pores, and finds the spaces between your skin to sink into. It heats you up like an oven and you can feel yourself growing weary in a very short time in the desert sun. Fortunately, we quickly spotted my father in his Eagle Talon, a car he bought for me but decided it fit him and his journey out west better, so he reclaimed it.

I carried the green army canvas bag Greg had given me for my travels and Beth had but one bag also, making it easy to collect our meager belongings. We then approached my father's car as he smoked cigarettes with the windows up. He watched us wait in the heat for our things. He didn't get out to greet us. I heard the door unlock as I neared.

"Hey guys," he said as we got into the car.

"Hi, Mr. Pete," Beth said. She patted his bald head from the back seat—her southern accent in full force.

"Hello, Father," I said. He didn't say anything but grabbed my hand and squeezed it.

Sucking the cigarette clenched tightly between his teeth, he shifted the small manual transmission car into first gear. We lurched forward toward the street, then sped away from the busses and the station. The ash of his cigarette fell on his chest with an ember still glowing.

"It's good to see you, Teen," (short for Tino, short for Santino), he finally said.

"Thanks for picking us up," I said as I stared at the countless scabs and burns from fallen cigarette ashes onto his forearms.

After a short drive, when we pulled into an RV park in South Scottsdale, I realized my mistake of coming to see him was a magnificent one. I scanned the RVs looking for my father's blue and white creeper van that he used to pull the trailer from California to Arizona. My heart sank when we turned a corner and I saw the van. Next to it was not a trailer or an RV, but more of a camper. A family spending the weekend in the mountains would find it acceptable, or a meth tweaker, but for Beth and I to live there, with my father? All I could think of was, "What the hell did I do? Fuck."

Beth looked at me with worried eyes as we exited the car. We brought our bags in and put them on the small beds in the back of the camper where we would be sleeping—Beth on one bed, me on the other, not for any other reason than the two of us wouldn't fit on a bed together. In between our beds and my father's, in the front of the camper, were a small kitchenette and dining table. The thick stench of cigarette smoke and ashes permeated the rooms. I was none too happy about that, as my father's incessant smoking in the house was one of the reasons he and I fought so much leading to his eventual departure from South Carolina.

The next day I went to Scottsdale Community College and enrolled in classes. I didn't have any money to pay for them, but since my father was a veteran, and I was a recipient of educational benefits because of his service, I was able to defer my tuition until my federal financial aid arrived. I then went in search of martial arts gyms that offered grappling classes.

In 2000, the popularity of Mixed Martial Arts (MMA), which was primarily responsible for bringing grappling martial arts to the masses, was pretty much still non-existent, but I had watched all of the Ultimate Fighting Championships on VHS or Pay-Per-View since the organization's inception in 1993, making me somewhat familiar with the sport.

It wasn't really my main intention to ever fight, but just a way to stay in shape and grapple so I could try to gain a spot on Arizona State University's wrestling team. In high school I was a pretty good wrestler. Not as good as I thought I was, but I was still rather decent. I went undefeated my senior year during the regular season, and the only time someone scored a point against me (except for an escape point—which doesn't really count) was when I got injured during one of my matches. I still won the match, but I did get scored on. A week before the state-qualifying tournament our team was training with another high school, and I injured my elbow pretty badly wrestling with one of their coaches. My dreams of becoming a state champion ended there. I was still able to compete, but with only one working arm I didn't make it to the podium, let alone win. When I lost my second match, kicking me out of the tournament, I went upstairs into the locker room and sat there for over an hour with tears streaming down my face. I was damned if I'd let that be my last wrestling match, though, and I made all efforts to wrestle in college in New York, but as we know, that didn't work out either.

I borrowed my father's car and canvased the Phoenix area for a place to train to stay in shape for wrestling season. I walked in (and quickly out) of many martial arts gyms, unsatisfied with their offerings. They were always housing some fat, white-haired or bearded Gandalf the Grey middle-aged man trying to convince me to train Wing-Chung Kung Fu, or Aikido, or some other nonsense. After five or six failed attempts I walked into a building that said *Brausa Academy* over the door and had stickers on the windows that read *Brazilian Jiu Jitsu, Grappling, MMA*. I knew I was in the right place.

There was a dark-haired, dark-skinned Cuban man (as I'd come to learn later) inside fumbling around with some wood beams that he seemed to be having trouble with. When he turned and saw me, he fumbled his words worse than the wood.

"Oh, oh, hi, yeah, can I help you?" he said.

"Um, I wanted to get some information about grappling classes," I said.

"Hi, I'm Roland. Yeah, come on in. Are you looking to fight?"

"Huh? Fight? Oh, I don't know. Maybe. But, I was just looking for somewhere to train so I can stay in shape for wrestling season."

"So, you're a wrestler, huh? I could choke you out."

"Oh, okay," I replied, worried that I'd come across a lunatic as I nervously stared back at him.

"No, really, I could choke you out fast. I'll squeeze your neck right off. I'm like an anaconda. At first you think you can breathe all right, but I keep squeezing, and I'll just get tighter and tighter. Ha ha, I'm just messing with you," he said as he chuckled and hit me on the arm.

"Come back tomorrow afternoon at four and train. I guarantee you'll love it. You'll be hooked," Roland said.

He was right. I was hooked. The next day when I went in to train, Roland singled me out of the class when the live training started and proceeded to strangle me time and again. He choked me out with such ease, with such frequency, I physically couldn't swallow solid food for two days. I signed up and I never competed in another wrestling match. I'd spent the last few years trying to obtain something I didn't know was out there. I thought it was wrestling, but it wasn't.

People always asked me why "fighting," though? Why didn't I pick professional tennis or become a pro dart player or bowler? I always told people it was about the competition of the sport, that it really puts life into perspective when you're in a situation where you are about to fight, hand to hand, against another trained human in front of a crowd, or that it was my lifelong dream of becoming a Ninja Turtle that funneled me toward fighting. I'm not so sure either is entirely true. Both are true—to a degree. I do hold that perspective on fighting, and if only I had been able to mutate into a pizza-eating turtle, all would have been perfect in my life. But I think my fighting career has more to do with my delusions of grandeur, mixed with a little megalomania, with a dash of fear of dying, and my desire to immortalize my name—even in some obscure sense—to avoid absolute death. I thought if people knew my name, I could achieve some level of success that could be considered greatness. I needed people to know my name.

On top of every rational thought I have given fighting, I am also drawn to the primal part of pugilistic endeavors. Men should fight. Men should hunt, and fish, and chew tobacco, and go camping. I don't hunt. I don't fish. I don't chew tobacco. I don't camp. I fight. I think we all need to fight a little more in life. Since my early adult years, I've always thought kids should fight in school—it's not like I'm asking for the Attica riots in every kindergarten classroom or anything—but I think kids need to let their fists fly to settle arguments every once in a while without the cops getting called. I think our society has become so passive that we freak out about everything, regardless of how minor it may be—not just in schools, but in general. A little playground fight here and there lets boys know there are repercussions for things they say and do. I'm not sure I would trust any man than can say he's never been in a fight. I'd ask him, "Why the hell not?"

The next best thing to punching people, though, may be choking them, and Roland was certainly allowing his dominant ancestral traits to be shown as his arms were wrapped around my neck. After Roland had had his way with my neck for the evening, and I was back at our trailer, I asked my father to open the window next to where he sat to let some of the smoke out.

"Teen, it's really hot outside. I don't want to let the cold air out," he said to me.

"Dammit! I knew I shouldn't have come here. Not a damn thing has changed. You're as selfish as you ever were," I said, in a tantrum, as I walked outside and slammed the door.

Beth came out to console me and said in her southern accent, "Don't worry, Santino. It's going to be all right. We won't be living here for too long." That night we moved our belongings into the back of my Father's creeper van. We slept in there from that point on. The nights were filled with sweat and discomfort and agitation. Beth never once complained, though I could tell by her hazel eyes she was very worried, wondering what she had agreed to.

I showed up the next day to train at Brausa Academy and learned of a fight that Roland was promoting that coming Thursday. When I told Beth about it she was nervous.

"Don't you think you should train a little while before you fight? I mean, I think you'll do just great, don't get me wrong, but has the other guy—the guy you'll be fighting—has he trained long?" she asked.

"I won't know until I show up. They don't know what fighters will be there until the day of the fight. It's normal for that to happen," I said, confidently, as if I knew a thing.

When Thursday finally arrived, and the excitement that clouded my head parted momentarily, I realized that I was surely unprepared for any sort of pugilistic endeavor. Forget about the fact that I had only been training for a week or two and had no idea how to fight—how to throw a proper punch, kick or defend either or that I barely knew a submission, or how to get out of one—forget about those miniscule details. But, I also realized that I didn't have the proper attire to entertain the crowd in. I didn't have any super stretchy spandex shorts that had intimidating animals on the sides, which, unfortunately for everyone involved, was the standard outfit for MMA fighters at the time. How was I supposed to win if I didn't even dress the part?

With my limited knowledge of my new sporting hobby, I went to the local mall in Scottsdale and scoured the stores for any type of shorts that might suffice. The mall, Scottsdale Fashion Square, is an upscale establishment and didn't have any type of sporting store, let alone a store that housed outfits for such an obscure sport. I was out of luck.

After pacing the mall for some time, about to accept defeat, I noticed a swim store—more specifically, a Speedo Store.

Shining like the sun's rays were illuminating them straight from God himself, hung a pair of black, white, blue, and yellow Speedo shorts.

I purchased a pair of the small, stretchy swim attire with money given to me from my father then spent the rest of the day trying to prevent bile from sneaking up my esophagus.

\* \* \*

Seeing the person approach the cage, my stomach flipped and turned like a gymnast at the Olympics. I bit down on my mouthpiece and pushed the four-ounce gloves onto my knuckles. There was my opponent. My first opponent ever. This was the beginning. I was ready.

I had been in fights on the streets many times before, but they usually just happened. Someone said something. Someone got mad. Punches were thrown. Fight ends. This was very different, though. This was planned. The planning took all of the rage and anxiety and adrenaline that would normally be present in a street fight and magnified them. The waiting let my emotions sit out in the desert sun, like an egg on the sidewalk, and cook. The wait seasoned and heightened every emotion I felt for days. And it gave the fear time to creep into my mind. In street fights the adrenaline and testosterone were always so high that the fear side of fighting never reared its ugly, cowardly face. With days to do nothing but play the scenarios out in my mind it gave me time to second-guess my decision to fight. After I weighed in and sat through the pre-fight rules meeting, the fear and adrenaline and excitement and rage swirled around and took their dominant turns with me, but now—now, even if I didn't think I was ready, there was nothing I could do about it. Ready or not, the cage door would shut, and I would do only one thing: fight.

Then I saw him walk through the cage door.

He was a bald man—shaved to the skin—with a goatee, but he was wearing clothes. He wore a pair of jeans and work boots and a black t-shirt that read

"Brausa Academy" on it. Clarity came back to my vision as I focused on his face and realized it was a man named Tom, a cage-side worker. *What the shit?*

"We don't know where your opponent is? They're trying to find him now. We think he left."

The MC called out his name a few more times, but he didn't show up. Tom came back into the cage and told me he was a no show and that maybe I'd have better luck next time. I was angry. I was relieved that it was over for the time being, but I was angry. It took every ounce of courage I had in every cell of my body to walk up to the cliff and jump and it turned out that the cliff was a mirage, and I could keep walking forever without ever falling.

Walking down the steps, Tom stuck his hands out. In them, a trophy.

"What is that for?" I asked.

"You still won. Technically it's a win for you since he no-showed."

"I didn't win shit," I said as I pushed the trophy out of my way. I immediately grabbed my sweatpants and put them on, covering my pale, skinny legs, and my small Speedo.

"Nice underwear, faggot," a woman yelled from the crowd as I passed her on my way back to the warm-up area.

# 3

Once I knew I could no longer fight, I started applying for jobs at various businesses immediately. Eventually I was able to land interviews at two financial firms: Morgan Stanley and Balboa Capital.

When I went in for my interview at Morgan Stanley-Dean Witter—and by having me there at all, I think it kind of diminishes the credibility of any financial advisor there—I made a point to mention to the secretary that my grandfather was Bill Saufley, the former long-time Vice President of the Dean Witter investment firm. She about flipped her wig, and gave me the royal treatment. During my initial interview screening, I was obligated to take some sort of mental capacity test—to see if I would be able to study and pass the series 7 securities exam. While taking the test, numerous people came in and asked, "Are you Bill Saufley's grandson?" To which I happily smiled and said, "Yes."

I was already counting my money in my new role as a stockbroker. I was more than happy when I went in to interview with the manager after I'd passed the initial-screening test.

"I don't like to hire people without college degrees. Means they haven't completed anything. I don't really care what degree it is, but a degree means someone's willing to see something out. See it through," the manager said.

*Did you not hear that I am the grandson of the beloved Bill Saufley?! Um, people outside are fawning over me!*

"Oh, I completely understand. I honestly had planned to finish school, but my career as an athlete and managing the gym were really taking off, and I had to choose."

"So, why are you leaving the gym now? You chose that career path over college?"

"Well, after my injury, I don't want to stay in that industry. I've always had an interest in the financial sector, because of my grandfather, you know. And I think it's about time for me to begin that path."

He didn't like me. He saw right through my bullshit, but, with trepidation, and after a few more phone calls from his secretary, he offered me the job.

"I'll give you a shot. I hope I'm not going to kick my own ass here."

And like that I was hired at Morgan Stanley.

"Sometime this week, send in copies of your w-2's from your last two years to verify your previous income, and we'll get this ball rolling," he said.

*Huh? Did I just hear that right? W-2's?*

"Oh, yeah, of course. I'll get those to you immediately," I replied.

And like that, I was un-hired from Morgan Stanley.

I knew I couldn't produce a legitimate W-2, or tax returns from my previous years working at Arizona Combat Sports, as they didn't exist. When I got home I conferred with Steve about the situation.

"No. No, you cannot falsify a W-2, Santino. That's like fraud or something. I'm sure that is illegal. Actually, if there's one document you don't want to falsify, it's anything that has to do with taxes and the IRS."

"How will they know? It's going to a company. They're not going to check with the IRS about things."

"You don't want to do it. Take the other job."

And I did.

The secretary at Morgan Stanley called me numerous times in hopes of acquiring the proper documentation from me to get me started there ASAP.

"Hi Santino, I'm just calling to get those W-2's faxed over, so we can start your new-hire paperwork. Please call me before the week ends."

A few days later:

"Hi, Santino, I still haven't heard from you and just wanted to remind you of the new-hire paperwork. Please call me back. Glad to have you on board!"

And yet, after the weekend:

"Well, Santino, we haven't heard anything from you. This is very disappointing that you have not gotten in contact with us. I was really excited to have you as a part of our team. Your grandfather would be very disappointed in the way you have handled this."

What was I to do, though? I couldn't out and tell her that my entire resume was a lie, and so I chose a job cold-calling businesses in hopes of getting them to take out capital loans and leases through Balboa Capital.

The job was putrid. I cold-called hundreds of businesses a day, and somehow got shot down and hung up on more times than I dialed. I sat in my cubicle and contemplated of the serenity a gun exploding my head could offer on a daily basis. The team leaders cheered on the new-hires with their slimy B.S. talk and made us think we'd all be millionaires. Sometimes, to meet the call quota, I'd call my cellphone twenty, thirty, fifty times a day and leave messages, or just hang up. At least then the managers wouldn't harass me about my calls.

One night, I was sitting in my bed reading and I felt a pounding in my head. The pressure built. It squeezed my brain inside its grip and assaulted, not only my brain, but my emotions. *Is this it? Is it all over now? Something must be going on with the aneurysm. I'm going to die. I know it, I'm going to die!*

I laid on the floor. My eyes blurred as I looked through their watery lenses. My chest swelled and heaved rapidly and choppily. After an hour or so, I realized my head hurt because I had a headache. The rest was my anxiety. The anxiety of my brain bursting. The anxiety of hating my new life. The anxiety of working for the shyster telemarketers. The anxiety of not realizing my dreams.

As I began to miss more and more work at Balboa, Steve's life was unraveling at a much faster pace than my own. He'd received another DUI a couple of weeks after the first, and his ex-girlfriend informed him that she was pregnant. His only option, as he saw it, was to sell his house, move to Thailand, travel to Nepal and climb Ama Dablam—a mountain in the Himalayan range across from Everest. At which point, I was forced to move from my beloved lair to a room with old friends that I trained with while fighting, Steve and Ray Steinbeiss.

Another move. Another lost friend. Still uncertain of what was to come.

# 4

**November 8, 2000:**

My *real* first cage fight was much less memorable. Three months after I first walked into Brausa Academy I finally had an opponent climb in the cage with me. The fellow's name was Joe Vensor and he was as inexperienced as I was. He was an amateur boxer, and a piss-poor one at that, which pleased me, as I was a wrestler, knowing he would be unable to defend my takedown.

A couple of the fighters from the gym, Shawn Upshur, and his brother, James, warmed me up and cornered me for the fight. Fortunately, I'd acquired the proper fighting attire since my last outing: a pair of black spandex shorts with white trim that was about halfway between the length of bike shorts and my previously poor choice of a Speedo. The shorts read "Brausa" on the back.

The excitement was almost more than I could bear when I saw Joe walking to the cage. I knew the fight was actually going to take place. Every cell, molecule, and atom in my body had been jumping around for days as if microwaves were heating me from the inside out in anticipation for the bout.

*Let's do this. I'm ready. He looks skinny.* The bell rang. I went straight for him. I pushed him against the cage where I landed a few body shots. *He's weak. Hit him some more. Get the takedown.* I squatted down and latched onto his legs, lifting him in the air. I turned him toward the middle of the cage and slammed him to the mat. *You're winning.* I had him pinned down and was beating the side of his head and ears when I looked over and saw Roland next to the cage yelling, "Choke him!" Then he motioned with his right arm how to put it under a neck and lock up a choke. *Huh? Oh yeah, choke him. Right. I need to choke him.* I followed his charade act and me the winner of the fight. Sadly, I lost, but in reality, anyone involved in the affair—from spectator to referee to judge—should get a loss in life included on his or her record for being anywhere near that debacle. Looking back, neither of us should have been in that cage.

During that first year of MMA, Beth and I were fortunate enough to escape the smoke storm that was my father's trailer. I got a job at a small electronics store in the mall and Beth worked at the front desk at a hotel close to the RV park. One day, when Beth was sick at work, her boss insisted Beth accept a ride home in her vomitus state. When her manager bore witness to our living arrangements at the RV park, sleeping out of the back of the van, she immediately demanded we move into the hotel for as long as we needed until we could procure our own apartment.

The first time we sat on the bed in our new room we exchanged giant smiles, and a sense of relief came over both of us, even if it was just a momentary reprieve from the world we were trying to conquer. We stayed in that moment as long as we could. It was like waking up on Christmas morning and unwrapping a gift that you wanted. We woke up on our Christmas morning and saw hope and a future.

\* \* \*

Our family barely had a penny. My father spent the majority of his welfare check and military disability on alcohol and cigarettes. Our food stamps were used to purchase copious amounts of deviled ham and deviled chicken, both in the can. But, we had a Christmas tree. We drove to the woods that my father still owned outside of Theresa, and spent the day cutting down, and subsequently dragging out, the largest pine tree we could find. When we got it home, Chea, Adrianna, and I—them much more than I—cut ornaments out of cardboard boxes and colored and decorated them with tin foil and crayons. After the tree was decorated, my sisters and I spent the next few weeks wrapping anything we could find in the house using newspaper: scissors, cars, dolls, rulers, protractors, gloves, socks, music tapes...anything.

Anything we found was wrapped. We placed our wrapped presents under the tree when the recipient wasn't near and scampered off with a smile and sense of satisfaction. Most of the presents were dressed in black and white attire from the newspaper, but there was the sporadic colorful outcast, noticeable and vibrant with sides flashing pictures of Charlie Brown or another comic. By the time Christmas came we could hardly walk through our living room without tripping over the gifts.

Adrianna and I sat under the tree for hours on end and guessed what the other had wrapped for days before Christmas came. She was out of school on break and I was just happy my sisters were home with me.

"It's scissors. I know it," she'd say.

"No it's not. You could guess all day and you won't figure it out."

"Well, do you know what this one is?" she'd ask.

"I bet it's a car. I can feel the wheels."

"You'll never be able to tell what it is. You'll just have to wait till Christmas morning to find out," Adrianna would say in the omnipresent condescending tone that an older sister is allowed to have. One that Chea never used.

The guessing was the greatest part. None of us cared what we got. We knew they were things we had. We knew we weren't going to get any new toys or clothes or even a good meal. We just loved the game of it all. When our faces either dropped because we had guessed wrong for those weeks, or lit up because we fooled someone, that was the greatest joy I have ever felt on any Christmas then or since. That was the moment. That was the moment when the blissful naivety of childhood was stronger, and more protective, than any worldly exposure. It kept us safe—me much longer than my sisters, who were older and forced to raise me. And if, by chance, we did get something new, something from Santa or a relative, the surprise would be even more exciting. Though that rarely happened, we never gave up hope. Even if we knew Santa only visited children in other homes. In homes unlike ours.

The Christmas glow did wear off during the evening, though, when my father told me he was going to throw my best friend, Topper, a stuffed cow, in the trash because I didn't clean my room well enough after we opened our presents. I sobbed for hours and my sisters hid Topper under their stuffed animals in their room so my father wouldn't find him. He never looked. Instead, he passed out on the couch—where he slept my entire life.

It was early in the night when Chea woke me and told me to come downstairs. It was after midnight and black inside my room. The draft from the window crept in. I was cold and didn't want to get out from my blankets.

"Come on, Tino. Dad wants us downstairs."

"Why? What's going on?" I asked.

"I don't know."

My father sat at the table. The bottle of whiskey next to the ashtray was well on its way to being emptied. We were directed to sit down. We sat in silence. My head drooped as the sleep began to take over again. BAM! The loud noise of my father's hand hitting the table startled me back to consciousness. I knew the drill. I wish I didn't. I wriggled in my chair. Shifted my weight back and forth. The coughing and choking and frustration of my child cry-fit began before the tears. My sisters tried to calm me. My father sat silent.

Eventually my cries stopped and acceptance took over. Eventually my father's head began to droop as the alcohol either strengthened or weakened—I'm not sure. His head on his arm, six little eyes shot back and forth at each other and the top of a head that lay on the table. We surreptitiously slid our chairs back. *Maybe he was asleep and we could escape?* His head popped back to attention and he glared at us through the fog of sleep and drink and PTSD. He lit another cigarette and sucked away—with plumes of smoke stringing through the air, he shot gusts of smoke through his nose like a dragon. The cat and mouse game continued through the night.

We sat awake, silent, until we saw the sun creep through the windows. As we stood and tip-toed away from the table, his head moved again. His eyes looked to and fro, but he didn't stop us. *We escaped.* The wooden stairs creaked as we climbed up toward our rooms. I melted in my bed.

It was well into the afternoon when I woke up. My sisters were already down in the kitchen while my father sat at the table.

"Hey, Tino," he said cheerfully.

I looked at my sisters. No alarms were sent my way.

He gave us the option to stay in the duplex in Watertown or move back to the woods in Theresa where we'd live in a trailer without electricity, running water, heat, or any other amenity that would suggest we lived in the twentieth century. "It will be like camping," he said. "And your mother won't be able to find us."

We voted unanimously to move to the woods.

We moved as soon as the snow melted. There's a reason children aren't allowed to purchase cigarettes or alcohol until adulthood. There's a reason children aren't allowed to vote or join the military. They don't understand what they agree to or the consequences of their actions.

We didn't understand the consequences of that decision. We soon would.

# 5

A few more weeks passed working at Balboa before I began the search for a new job. Eventually I landed a gig as a banker for Chase Bank. Kindal and I were becoming more serious, and I spent most of my time with her, and barely any nights at my room with the Steinbeiss brothers. But I was bored. I had to wear a tie to work every day, which I know is nowhere near the worst thing that can happen in life, but I was bored with ties. I was bored with selling things to people. I didn't want to call people anymore in hopes of earning their business, or their money. It was the same reason Steve Hyatt had left and gone off the grid. We weren't used to being tied down. We weren't used to structure and monotony. I yearned for enlightenment and excitement and the travel schedule that I had while I was fighting. Gallivanting across the country and meeting new people and going to other countries and witnessing other cultures and seeing the world from a different lens.

Eventually, Kindal and I moved in together and we rented a house in South Scottsdale after drinking too much wine and thinking the house was "perfect." It certainly was not with its 1960's original turquoise stove and oven and old worn carpets and rickety old closet doors. It definitely looked much nicer under the veil of too many Pinot Noirs, but it worked. Her, me, and our Blue Pitbull, Atticus, were one happy family. I found a new job, again. This time, I found a company that I could work for that didn't have me selling anything to anyone! I was an institutional record keeper for Vanguard, a financial investment firm.

That meant I made changes to members' employee accounts (IRA's, 401k's etc.). When someone wanted to change what retirement funds they allocated money to, I made the changes. When someone wanted to take a loan out from their IRA or 401k, I processed that. And so on and so forth.

My tenure began on the first working day of 2006, and from that very first day of training, I had health insurance. I could finally receive the brain surgery needed to rid myself of that pesky aneurysm taunting my anxiety-riddled brain.

Life at Vanguard was much better than life at Balboa or Chase, and outside of the formal dress code (dress pants, dress shirt, and tie...even in the summer!) it was a pleasurable experience. The people were nice, professional. But, most of all Vanguard provided me with a stable income, something I'd never had as a fighter, and for that, I was more than happy to enter my cube and sit on my growing fat ass.

People don't think about the struggle with dreams enough. The times where you have negative dollars in your bank account with zero gas in your car that doesn't have insurance and all you want to do is eat a .99-cent item off of a dollar menu but you're .49 cents short of that. Or when you're sleeping on the mats in gyms or on friends' couches or wondering how you're going to pay for dinner and a movie with the new dream girl you have a date with, and your jaw's wired shut. Nope. People think about making it. They think about the good times—the highs, but there are a lot of valleys on the way to the top of those tall peaks. Working for Vanguard, I didn't find myself with an adrenaline filled smile at the top of those peaks, but I also didn't find myself at the bottom of those depression-filled valleys, either. So there was that.

After the checks had come in for a few weeks, Kindal and I went to a Nordstrom Rack store in North Scottsdale to pick out some new work shirts for me. When I looked down at my vibrating phone and saw my sister Adrianna's number looking at me, I answered.

"Tino, where are you?" Her voice cracked. I could hear the pain.

"What's wrong? What's going on?"

"Dad's dead."

"What? What—"

"Aunt Beth found him a couple of hours ago. They say his heart just gave out and he died at the table."

Before I could exit the store I was in tears. Our relationship was beyond tumultuous, but he had always been there. Even if he wasn't helping in any capacity. But, physically, he'd always been somewhere where I could see him. He was the only constant in my wild life. We'd moved so many times. There were so many schools. I didn't know my mother or almost any family, for that matter. My friends changed with each new town or school, but him, he was always there. Hell, even my sisters were grown up and living their own lives, but my father was still sitting there at the kitchen table, alcohol replaced by prescription pain meds and benzos and tranquilizers—arms still burned from the cigarettes. But he was there. Sitting. Waiting. Always there when I needed him to be there. Always there when the whirlwind of life was too chaotic. Always there when I needed something, someone grounded in my life.

Until he wasn't.

I was more uncertain than ever. When I lost fighting, I didn't know what I would do with the rest of my life. When I lost my father, I didn't know where my life was. I didn't know anything. I'd never had a "home". We moved too much, but I always knew where home was where my father was, regardless of whether I liked it or not.

# 6

**May 3, 2002:**

I turned professional about a year after my first amateur fight. My opponent, Del Hawkins, was from one of the rival gyms called *The Dawg Pound*. He was nicknamed the Filipino Delight. It's easy to figure out where the Filipino comes from, but as for the Delight, well, that's what imaginations are for. He was a loudmouth. He always yapped like a little barking Chihuahua about his upcoming opponents and thought he could defeat Gojira himself if confronted with the beast. He was also missing one of his front teeth, which made me think less of him for that. During our fight, I rag-dolled the "Delight" for three rounds, but couldn't find a way to put the defiant bastard away, and earned a unanimous decision victory for the win. I earned a mind boggling $35 dollars for the affair—the minimum a professional had to be paid per the new Boxing Commission rules that had just begun regulating our sport. I cashed it and went to Denny's.

Next up was a wrestler named Adam Durant. Roland had asked me to fight him a day before the show, and I hesitantly accepted. Initially, I declined the bout. I had been sick for days and didn't want to compete.

"Hey, Franco, I'm glad you're here. I got a great fight for you for tomorrow," he said as I walked into Brausa. I had been sick, but I stopped in to say hi as I was near the gym.

"I don't think I'll be any good for tomorrow. I've been sick. That's why I haven't been in."

"Oh, don't worry about that. You'll crush this guy. He's just a wrestler. He doesn't know anything else. You'll finish him in the first round."

"Can we fight on the next card?" I asked, knowing the answer.

"You know, never mind. Don't worry. The whole fucking card is falling apart. I'll find someone to fight him. But, you know, you're missing a big opportunity here."

Defeated, I said, "I'll fight him. I'll be there tomorrow, and I'll fight him."

"You're going to do great, Franco. This guy's no good."

I woke at the cusp of dawn to a calm day. There was nothing alarming about the morning as my eyes introduced themselves to the light that crept through the cracks in my window shades. The clouds in my head from being sick numbed me from the reality that there was a fight looming. There was a storm that evening, and I was left outside without a raincoat or umbrella. My eyes were leaking fluids and I was sneezing, so I gobbled up a few Sudafed and vitamin C and felt more human after the meds kicked in. I spent most of the day resting in my bed to save my energy. I barely thought about the battle that night. It was out of reach. Out of the reach of my mind to conceive such a thing given the amount of cotton between my ears. It was strenuous to think of the fight that waited for me just beyond the reach of my psyche, so I thought about sleep. I blew my nose incessantly and dabbed my eyes with toilet paper.

After I weighed in that evening, I continued to lie down and think of anything but pugilism. There were so many things on my mind that didn't involve hitting or strangling others of the same species. There were dreams of warm beaches and delusions of grandeur that weren't going to fulfill themselves. There was a myriad of unintelligible thoughts that ranted and raved through my ears and mind until a couple of fights before mine.

I was the eighth fight on the card and, at some point, some training partner must have informed me of my need to warm up, so I acquiesced to his demands, but not before eating a couple more Sudafed to help me reach a state of clarity, which pepped me up a bit, too. Then I drank a cup of coffee for good measure. When I started shadow boxing I was amped and my sickness was a mere afterthought.

Rage in the Cage, our fight promotion, had upgraded from dingy bars in South Phoenix to real venues, and the crowds were typically around two thousand at that point. When they announced my name, I fought my way through the clouds of fake smoke and emerged into the roaring arena as a fan favorite since I was announced as fighting out of the Brausa Academy, one of the better gyms in the state.

I saw Durant standing in the cage pacing and jumping up and down to stay warm. He was a light-skinned black man who wrestled at Embry Riddle Aeronautical University in Prescott, Arizona. He was tall and lean like me. I no longer felt sick, and I stared at him through the chain-link as I neared. Feeling shitty all day had curbed my nerves and I was happy to have them leave me alone before a fight for once. For the first time of any of my fights, I wasn't afraid at all. There were no nerves that made my stomach bulge or my balls drop with the anxiety of adrenaline. I walked to my corner, took a sip of water and turned toward him as the door of the cage closed. The referee gave us our last instructions and yelled, "Fight!"

He came at me fast with a flurry of punches. I caught them on the arm and circled. *He's fast. Circle. Move right.* I threw a low kick that landed and he bulldozed me over onto the mat. *He's strong. Grab the wrist. Shoot your legs up for the triangle choke.* He punched me in the eye socket while I was on my back. *Hold him. Wrap up his arms so he can't hit you.* I grabbed him and pulled him into me, but he was strong. He knew what he was doing and we were sweaty. He kept sliding out of my grip like a fish in my hands in the water. *Go to the arm bar or Kimura* (shoulder lock.) He held me down until the end of the round. The bell rang and I went back into my corner.

I stood with my fingers through the chain-link above my head to try to get my breath. I had anvils in my arms and legs. They felt heavy. They just wouldn't move. I got water from my corner and turned back around toward Durant, who was bouncing up and down like a fucking jackrabbit. He had energy for days. I was wheezing, but I was still standing. We still had two more rounds.

The bell rang and we were center cage again. I threw a jab-cross combination and he once again steamrolled me onto the canvas. My head was pinned against the chain-link and his forearm. *I have to finish this. I think I only have one burst left. Fuck, he's strong! Kick him off. Get on top.* I put my heels on his hips and kicked. He flew backwards and I sat up and shot in on him to take him to the mat. He sprawled and spun around me. His arm wrapped around my neck. *You're good. He doesn't have his hooks in* (feet locked around me.) *It's tight. Shit. Tap.* The fight was over.

I stayed on the mat for a few seconds before I got up. My face was hot and my body weary. His hand went up in victory as my head fell in defeat.

Roland told me he wasn't any good and that I'd crush him. Well, he was good, and I didn't crush him. Forty-two seconds into the second round of my second professional fight and I had a loss on my record. I was only two fights into my professional career, and I had a .500 record. Amateur losses don't mean anything. They get erased when you go pro, but professional losses never go away. It's not like we have a season and get to reset our records every year at 0-0. They are with us for a lifetime. Wherever my name goes, Adam Durant's victory over me will follow. If this were boxing, my career as a prospect would have ended at that forty-second tick of the clock when I tapped out.

After the fight I sat at a diner with Beth and wondered if I was supposed to be there. *Was I cut out to be a professional fighter?*

I didn't show up to the Brausa Academy for a week. It was by far the longest I had gone without going into the gym. I didn't want to see the people in there that expected me to win. I didn't want the condolences. I didn't want the looks in their eyes letting me know they understood my pain and that it was going to be okay. I wanted to think about my road, and if the path to greatness went through MMA.

When I did go in it was exactly as I had expected it to be.

"Don't worry about that, man. We all lose at some point."

"You'll be back on track fast."

"I just feel sorry for the next guy you fight!"

They went on and on. I needed a week to have my tantrum, and I had it. But then I decided MMA was something I was going to pursue. After days of pissing and moaning about it, Beth finally said, "You can do anything you want, Santino. If you want to make it as a professional fighter, you can do it. If you want to do anything else, you can do that, too. I believe in you." She was my Adrian. And I her Rocky.

She was right. I could make it as an MMA fighter. Some of the other guys were right, too. My opponents after Durant should have been worried. I started to rack up the wins.

\* \* \*

A year and a few apartments later I was still attending Scottsdale Community College—more for the veteran's benefits I received than an education—and training three to four hours a night while Beth worked at the hotel and lived a life that orbited my own. Over time Beth and I started to grow apart. We had grown bored with one another. I was spending my time training and fighting, and was more interested in MMA than a relationship at the time; she was tired of my constant absence from the house due to my training schedule, and wanted someone that held her as a higher priority than I did. Eventually, we decided to split up.

Like many of the women throughout my life, Beth was always there for me. She was the same woman when I had money or when I searched through the couch cushions for coins to buy something off of the dollar menu. She loved me. Unconditionally. She supported me, and my career as a fighter, while I collected a government check from the Veterans Administration, for going to school. She nurtured me. She mothered me. She fawned over me. She was everything a man could ever want in a woman, but she just wasn't the right woman for me. Our three-and-a-half year relationship eventually came to an end. I only spoke with her a handful of times after she left for the East Coast.

Begrudgingly, I moved back into my father's new house (that was an actual house and void of my sisters at the time) while I wheedled my way into a more permanent, less smoky, living arrangement.

# 7

I kept working, trying to keep my mind on Kindal and my future. Then, in March of 2006, I scheduled my brain surgery, or procedure—whatever it is called, as they didn't actually cut my brain or skull open, though there was still quite a significant risk of health-related issues with the procedure. An interventional radiologist named Dr. Cameron McDougal proceeded to cut a centimeter-length incision in my femoral artery (in my groin) and inserted a series of catheters. From my femoral artery, the catheters traveled up my body, through my heart, and into my brain, where Dr. McDougal placed coils into my aneurysm that keep the blood out. Then he placed a titanium stent into my carotid artery to keep the coils in place. My sister, Adrianna, and Kindal waited for just over six hours for the procedure to finish.

As the lights flickered on in my brain, I looked up at the lights in the elevator. I couldn't move my arms, legs, or head. I fought with all of my might to move, but nothing worked. When I looked over to my right, I saw my sister.

"Hey, I know you."

I then looked to my left and saw Kindal.

"And I know you too. How funny is that?"

"You've said that about a hundred times, now," Adrianna said as her and Kindal laughed.

"Why can't I move?"

The female nurse standing in the elevator with us spoke up. "You really made it tough for us. As we were waking you up, you pulled the catheters out of your leg and ripped your femoral artery. You sprayed blood all over the place. Took us a long time to fix it and stop the bleeding. It was pretty bad and we couldn't get you to calm down, so we had to strap you down."

"Probably a good idea," I replied.

The fog of the anesthesia was so thick that my brain had a hard time processing even the most basic commands and thoughts and actions. Once I got settled into my room and the nurse came in to shoot me full of morphine, I quickly snapped, "No! No morphine. No drugs. I need clarity. I need clarity, right now!" But then I shifted my weight and pulled onto the freshly bandaged, bloody groin and cried out in pain, "Give me the morphine. Give me the morphine." And the candy lady happily obliged my indulgences. When I was released from the hospital a couple of days later, I was prescribed blood thinners for thirty days, but other than the regular checkups with the doctor, there were no other major complications with the surgery.

Vanguard stayed the same: I showed up, they paid me. It was fine, but it was time for another change, though. But this time it wasn't a new job, it was a change in familial ties. My father had a small life insurance policy through FERS, the Federal Employee Retirement System, that left me with a few thousand dollars, and my sisters and I split the money from the sale of his house, so I had enough to purchase an engagement ring for Kindal.

She was out of town for a few days for work (She worked for a major pharmacy, setting up corporations with pharmacy benefit plans), and I had the ring shipped to the house, but since nobody was there to sign for it, the driver took the package with him. Damned if I'd allow a UPS driver to foil my proposal, I left work at two in the afternoon and went on the hunt for the driver. I called UPS repeatedly and told them the situation, and they tried calling the driver to have him go back to my house, but were unsuccessful. I drove around all the neighborhoods near my house, hoping to spot him, but to no avail. It was nearing seven at night and I still didn't have a ring, and with Kindal set to arrive at nine o'clock at night, my proposal was looking more and more like it would have to be delayed.

Like a scene out of a movie, though, just as I was pulling into my house a defeated man, UPS called me and told me the driver had brought the package back to the warehouse and that I could pick it up from them in their after-hours center. A few people even stayed late on their shifts to help me out. I didn't care how it happened, but it did. I got the ring!

I raced home to prepare my scene, which I was later informed was a major fire hazard and could have burned down the house. All over the house, I placed lit tea-light candles to set the mood. On the table was a box with a shirt from her favorite store, Anthropologie, inside. Under the shirt was the small, opened engagement ring box.

"Is everything okay?" Kindal asked as I picked her up from the airport. My hands sweating. My body trembling.

"Oh, yeah. Of course."

I then proceeded to drive home maniacally, to which she immediately took note of our glowing house.

"What's wrong with our house? Are those candles?"

This was not turning out to be as suave and romantic as it had all gone down in my head. *Damn!*

When she opened the box she was so happy to see the shirt and its origin. She then spotted the ring inside and threw the box and its remaining contents across the room and screamed.

*That's not a good sign. No, that can't be a good sign.*

I froze stiff. She froze stiff, but snapped out of it quickly and rushed to the ring and swiped it up from the floor. When she looked at me, my body remained frozen except for my eyes that grew to the size of saucers. We locked eyes, but said nothing.

*Oh shit. I'm supposed to propose!*

"Um, will you marry me?" I vomited out in the least enticing manner possible.

*Dammit, I forgot to get on a knee. I didn't even get on a knee. She can't say yes to me if I didn't even propose properly. Idiot.*

"Yes, of course I will."

*Really?*

# 8

**October 2003:**
Joe Riggs and I were set to land in Honolulu, Hawaii, where we were to compete at Rumble on the Rock, an MMA show run by former UFC lightweight and welterweight champion BJ Penn. And, once again, Joe was going off on rants that made me question my sanity.

Most people love Hawaii. Most people enjoy the relaxing scenery or the beach or whale watching or whatever it is most normal people do to relax while vacationing. But, most people aren't traveling with Joe Riggs. After we landed, we found our way to the hotel room in Waikiki. We were sharing a room and after we put our things away we were lying on our respective beds.

"You're out of your mind, aren't ya, Frank?"

"Nah. I'm feeling pretty good about this fight."

"Really? You're telling me you aren't scared at all? You're a better man than I. A better man, indeed, Frank."

After a few moments pause, and apparently unsettled by the fact that I seemed somewhat more sane than he was hoping, he felt the need to continue his infiltration of my psyche. He stood up off of his bed and asked, "What happens if you go out there and *BAM!* one punch to the jaw and down you go?" then he made a squealing noise like a pig, and fell face down on his bed. We laughed and decided we'd be better off perusing the beach and everything in our vicinity that wasn't the inside of our heads, and into the Hawaiian sun we went.

We spent the next couple of days holed up in our room and occasionally walked the streets of "paradise" in the evenings to watch people, mostly the hookers. There were always plenty of hookers meandering the streets the second the sun slid out of sight. They'd walk up to potential Johns in front of the police without batting an eye, but would make sure their chests were as plump and visible as could be. Joe and I looked on at these street walkers with a sense of disgust mixed with a lot of curiosity, but that fire was quickly stamped out after Alexander Oxendine told us there was a high rate of transsexual prostitutes, and that "you couldn't tell the difference a lot of the trannies and real women." We were as scared straight as kids being brought to a jail for an afternoon in hopes of turning them on a better path in life.

I was set to fight Deshaun Johnson, and Joe was fighting David "Kawika" Pa'aluhi. Deshaun was clearly the lesser-known of the two. Running into the locals involved with the MMA scene, we were frequently asked who our opponents were. It seemed our friend, Kawika, was a goddamn legend on the islands since whenever the name was mentioned the "Ooohs" and "Ahhhs" were spewed out in full force. "You're fighting Kawika? You're crazy, bra. Kawika throws cracks, brah!" One group of guys said in the hotel lobby as they looked Joe up and down.

"What? Is this guy spawned from Zeus himself?" I asked Joe.

"Ah, Kawika Pa'aluhi!" Joe squawked and lurched his head side to side as if taking a shot to the dome. "Shit, Frank!"

The day before we were set to weigh in for our pugilistic endeavor I spent a few hours training with Ron Jhun, Kai Kamaka, and crew at 808 Fight Factory—a place I used to train at while living on the gym floor for a summer the year prior. Joe refused to join me as Kawika trained at their "sister" gym "Jesus is Lord" which was the home of Bozo Palling and Ray "Bradda" Cooper along with Pa'aluhi. So, I traveled inland alone, away from the coast, to a small training center on the second floor of an industrial complex.

When I arrived, I saw Kai standing out front of the gym; the bay doors were rolled up at both 808 Fight Factory and Jesus Is Lord, their immediate neighbor. Kai was on the phone yelling at someone.

"Hey, brah, he want licks, I lick him," Kai said into the phone.

Confused by the strange words I waited.

"You tell him he fo' wan' come down da kine I give him licks. You know da kine, L and L. Fuck, brah," he said then hung up the phone. *Right! "Licks."* I thought. *He wants to kick someone's ass!*

"Ah, Tino!" Kai said as he hugged me. He explained to me the reason for requesting to "lick" someone and brought me into the gym to train. I didn't really want to "train." I was just hoping to roll for a bit to help my weight out, but when Kai told me Takanori Gomi and Genki Sudo, two MMA legends, were next door training with Bradda and crew, I wanted to go over and watch them work out for a while. Genki was THE man at the time—and will most likely stay that way until eternity falls. And, Gomi was stomping fools out in Shooto for a while at that point and was there to fight

BJ. Penn in the biggest non-title fight under 170lbs outside the U.F.C. I could ever imagine.

I went next door and sat watching the two Japanese icons rolling with the Hawaiian students of both Jesus is Lord and 808. After the round ended, Genki asked me if I'd like to roll. Nervously, I obliged. I sat to my guard and Genki slid a knee through to pass. I quickly threw my legs up and clinched a triangle choke around his neck. He tapped and gave me a big smile.

"Ah, very good," he said.

We continued our roll, but this time I stood up and we began to go for takedowns. I shot in on a single leg and Genki blasted his hip into my head. It was like running into a steel beam. He shucked me to the floor then knee barred me with little effort. He then passed my guard with the slickest move I'd ever seen. I asked him what he did, and he spent five minutes explaining every detail to me in broken English. Thirty minutes later, I decided I'd rolled enough as my calves and feet were cramping uncontrollably.

"Thank you very much for training with me," I said. Then I bowed to him. "I should stop training now, I am fighting Saturday and I'm cramping badly."

"You are fighting?" he questioned. "On same fight?" he pointed to Gomi, and I shook my head yes.

"You will win. I am very sure. You are very good," he said in broken English.

Thankful for the compliment, I bowed again and made haste back to the hotel. For some reason, I felt validated. I was actually good in that moment. A world-renowned fighter told me so—so it must be true. It was the first time I'd trained with someone that had really "made it" and I knew that meant that I would eventually "make it." I was now fighting on a big show in Hawaii—one of the biggest cards in the world, featuring one of the best fighters in the world: BJ Penn. It was big. I didn't know how big at the time, but I knew it was a big opportunity.

On fight night, when we arrived at the arena we were shown to our warm-up room, which housed most of the non-Hawaiians. There was Antonio Banuelos, Dennis Hallman, Gil Castillo, the largest 145lber ever in Gil Melendez and a few others along with Joe and I. Takanori Gomi and his corner, Genki Sudo, as well as the rest of their entourage, were lucky enough to have negotiated a private room and were nowhere to be seen.

I was third on the card. I was still unknown enough to be early on the undercard. The show was big, but I certainly wasn't. I was just a Haole boy being booed on his way to the cage. When the fight started, we met in the center of the ring.

I threw a right kick at my opponent's dark body. It missed. I shot in for a takedown. He shrugged me off effortlessly. *He has better hips than I thought. His wrestling's better than I expected.* I forced him to the cage. *Grab the legs and get the takedown.* I tried to pry my arms loose and grab his legs. He moved off the cage. *Damn. I need to get him down.* I shot in for another takedown. I didn't get it. I pulled guard and found the fight on the ground where I wanted it. I reached for a heel hook leg-lock. *He won't get out of this.*

*Crack! What was that? That was something bad. Something bad just happened.* I rolled over and tapped out. I didn't know why I tapped, but I tapped. Something hit my skull and I knew the damage was severe.

My head laid on the canvas floor while I sat on my knees—as if I were praying toward Mecca. I was confused. The lights were bright and I couldn't make sense of the cacophony in my brain. When I sat up I saw the blood on the canvas. On my hands. Kai was yelling at the ref. *What happened?*

I got up and walked to Kai, who was still yelling at the referee.

"Don't worry, bro, You won," Kai said?

"What? What do you mean?"

"That knee's illegal! This ain't Pride rules. You got the win. He's DQ'd."

Let me just say, Genki Sudo is no Nostradamus. He didn't know what the hell he was talking about with his fight predictions. I guess I did win my fight—but only because two illegal knees smashed into my face while I was on the ground -- shattered my orbital, my sinus cavity, and split my face open just under my left eye. I won due to the disqualification, but I'm not so sure I would have won if that knee hadn't landed. When it hit me, it felt like my soul had been damaged.

Phil Baroni, the ex-UFC champ and Rumble on the Rock color commentator, then interviewed me in front of a booing crowd and ridiculed me. "So, did that knee even cause any damage, or were you just looking for a way out or something?" As the blood ran down my face, I don't know what I said, but didn't want to be in that cage anymore. I was confused. I didn't lose, but did I really win? I didn't fight, and I didn't have an answer for an opponent with a mediocre record. Could I have won? Maybe, if I found my legs wrapped around my opponent's neck with a triangle choke, but I don't believe that would have been the case, and I didn't I think that then.

As we were walking back to the locker room, Kai said, "Man, that's some cheap shit. You would have kicked his ass easy, had that cheater not thrown that knee."

"Yeah, I know."

When I got back to the locker room, the doctor told me he thought my nose was broken along with my orbital bone. I didn't know what that really meant, but figured it couldn't be good. I then went looking for Joe, who was set to fight soon.

I asked one of the workers at the show, "Where's Joe? He's up soon?"

"Hey, brah, Joe jump off da roof."

"Huh?" I asked and leaned an ear in for a better catch of the response.

"Yeah, brah. He jump off da second floor onto the parking lot."

"No fucking way," I said in disbelief.

I ran to the parking lot and saw a crowd of people huddled into a circle. There was an ambulance near them with its lights flashing. As I got closer I could see Joe lying on the ground in a small puddle of his own blood with a neck brace on. *"Holy shit! He really did jump*!

"What the hell happened?" I asked Joe.

"Ah, dammit, Frank. I went down. Down like a plane in the sea."

"Did you jump off the roof?"

"Huh? No, I didn't jump off the damn roof, friend, but now I wish I had. I was warming up doing wind sprints in my flip-flops and one of the edges caught and sent me down."

"Why were you doing wind sprints in your sandals?" I asked.

"Ah, you know. Why do I do anything I do? This is ridiculous, Frank."

"What? Your neck or your life?"

"Both, friend. Both." The EMTs then loaded him into the ambulance and off he went.

As Joe was whisked away, I went back to the locker room to get stitched up by the oldest living medical practitioner I'd ever seen. His Parkinson's hands shook like a 9.0 quake as he sewed my face up while my head rested on a dirty focus mitt. There wasn't any lidocaine, so I had to make due with a needle being woven in and out of my face with my senses intact. Each prick of the metal that pierced my skin and flesh felt like the knee hitting again and again. *What the fuck am I doing?*

While recovering from the geriatric doctor, I sat alone on a curb behind the Blaisdell Center. I wasn't just alone in the present, I was pretty alone back in Phoenix. I'd left my old training situation. Beth had moved back East. A girl I started dating, and really fell for, Jonelle, moved back to Oregon. I'd started dating a new girl, Angie, but that was more out of not having a better option than actually enjoying the relationship. I'd flown out to Hawaii, with Joe, a friend, but not a coach.

My thoughts of loneliness were interrupted by the slaps of skin hitting the pavement in repeated succession. When I looked up, I saw someone sprinting down the street through the traffic and then into the parking lot. The figure headed directly toward me. Barefoot, wearing only fight shorts, with blood streaks on his arm and face, Joe was back.

"Frank, I'm back. Tell them I'm back. I can fight," he said, winded and looking like a total lunatic. His eyes were wide and his hands were trembling.

"Joe, I don't think they're going to let you fight."

As one of the workers approached us asking how Joe was doing, Joe again blurted out—this time to the worker, "I'm back. Let me fight."

"You can't fight, you have a concussion. What the hell's wrong with you?"

Other workers came up, and eventually JD Penn put the last nail in the coffin and told Joe he would not be fighting that night. Joe's eyes drooped like a beaten dog, and he walked away. Later that evening, as we all waited to get paid, Joe convinced me to do his bidding for him.

I walked up to get my check and asked, "Joe was wondering if he'd get his show money?" They looked at each other and the group started violently laughing and looking at around at one another and JD said to me, "But he didn't show!"

I then walked to the hospital to get my eye looked at before I got on a plane. I was worried that the pressure on the airplane would harm my eye and brain if my orbital was damaged too badly. The emergency room was filled with the coughing sicknesses and screaming babies along with the drunken asshole that every hospital across the world is filled with at midnight. After I checked in the E.R. I sat outside on the curb. I didn't want to be around those inside. Nothing good could have come from it.

The air was moist and warm, but when the breeze blew across my face it somehow cooled my swollen eye and my nerves. Again, I was alone, sitting on a curb in front of a hospital in Hawaii with my face swollen and bruised purple and green. I had been humiliated on the microphone by Phil Baroni, as he had questioned my intent to fight in front of 10,000 roaring Hawaiians. I laid down on the grass behind me and closed my eyes. My mind was silent for nearly an hour before I heard the Japanese voices near me. When I sat up, I saw two Japanese men in warm-up gear. They were Gomi's corner men.

The younger one had a bag of McDonald's food in his hand and was dividing its contents between himself and the older man he was with. The older man went into the hospital and the younger stayed outside. He looked at me and, maybe recognizing my Tapout shorts or some other fighter-defining characteristic and said, "You fighter?"

"Yes," I replied.

"Oh, very good."

He sat next to me and offered me French fries and half of his meal, even his drink. He only spoke a few words of English and I spoke absolutely no Japanese, but we sat there for hours and talked about fighting and life by pointing to things and pantomiming our way through our thoughts as we transcended verbal language and found ourselves communicating with one another in the most impossible way. We laughed about a surfer that the Japanese man had seen fall off of his board and run scared out of the tame waves at Waikiki. We joked about scarring people with my swollen eye. We were somber when discussing both my loss and Gomi's. At nearly four in the morning, though, my Japanese friend for the day left as his pupil, Takanori Gomi, was released from the hospital. When my friend left, I sat there, again, without anyone else, but I didn't feel as alone anymore.

I was also ready to leave. Even though my spirits and loneliness were lifted, I was exhausted. I went back into the E.R. to see how long it would be before a doctor saw me and they still didn't know. I decided to leave and go to my hotel room to sleep.

"If you have a major brain injury and you leave, you could possibly die," the receptionist said.

"I could die out there on the lawn waiting to be seen."

# 9

When I was in the seventh grade, Chea was still very quiet, though she spent much of her time away from home with the few friends she did have. I saw Adrianna only in passing for years. We spoke little, and she was happy about that. She was a self-righteous good-girl who was in with all the crowds that one was supposed to be in with in high school. I was the maniacal partier who fought boys of all ages, was having sex, hooking up with every girl in sight, and finding my way into drugs and trouble.

Starting with my sisters, who gave up their childhood so I could keep mine, it was the girls in my life that eventually moved me toward a more stable direction.

Chea was an athletic girl. She ran track through most of her high school career as a sprinter, and even made it to the state championships. Chea ran the one hundred, two hundred, and four by one hundred meters. Her thighs rippled like a cheetah when she ran, and Adrianna and I marveled at her, wondering how her athleticism was created out of our genetic code. Her athletic build was a stark contrast to her painfully shy personality. She needed braces badly growing up. I'm certain that contributed to her shyness, but I don't think all of the blame can be given to her teeth.

She was always quiet and alone, even when we were young. Along with being the genetically gifted physical specimen out of our lot, she was also our Mother Theresa. First, she acted like our mother and raised me, and to a lesser extent, Adrianna. She cooked and cleaned, and bore the burden of our father's wrath when it flared. She also bore the burden of waking me up and getting me ready for school—I followed in my father's tyrannical dislike of being woken. He for PTSD and nightmares of Vietnam, me for being cranky in the morning. Chea took the verbal beatings from our father that I never had to take, as I was daddy's little Tiger. Yet she never harbored any animosity toward Adrianna or me.

She turned one cheek, then the other, and repeated the cycle as long as she needed to; her emotional endurance outlasted her physical speed. Chea was kind. Adrianna and I have always had a biting, stinging tongue that Chea never got. She will stop traffic in rush hour to run across five lanes of cars to give a homeless man money or food or whatever she has. She always gives them the benefit of the doubt that they aren't drug addicts, but truly hungry or stranded and in need of gas.

She is kind to a fault and will let others take advantage of her. She is kind to the point where she will lose money and time and peace of mind for the sake of kindness, but she never waivers. She held the hair back of the girls that drank too much at parties in high school instead of having fun herself, and she continues to hold doors for those on the other side of the parking lot. I doubt that will ever change. I could also talk with Chea about anything and not worry about the judgments that would come from my other sister.

Adrianna was the antithesis of Mother Theresa, and, on the surface at least, Chea. She had little compassion for those with problems and held everyone accountable for their actions. Now, that's not to say that she lacks compassion as a whole, but she is very thrifty with whom she bestows it upon.

Adrianna was the brains in our family. She was the winner. She was smart, pretty, popular, and fashionable—even with the limited budget our father had us on. She somehow figured out life before the rest of us. She knew how to shop on a budget, but look sophisticated. She knew how to skip school and get straight A's in her Advanced Placement classes and make high honor roll. She once missed 60 days of school in a single year and still had stellar academic marks. Most of all, though, she knew that high school, even while in the midst of the action, was only a fragment of our life and that it didn't matter. Adrianna was ahead of our time.

In high school, Adrianna began dying her hair red—fire red. She's 5' 2" tall, though she will claim 5' 2 ¾" to her deathbed. Like Chea and me, she has blue eyes, but with my fair skin, as opposed to Chea's olive tone. She has a very strong jaw line and a thick neck and an Italian nose like our father's and mine. She looks like the much more attractive female version of myself. Well, at least that's what we were told in high school.

She was a popular girl in school, and remained a popular one until she no longer wished to associate with that crowd. One day, there was some sort of childish drama that middle and high school girls engage in and she snubbed the whole group. She's the only person I've ever known to turn down the "in crowd." And she did so with her nose in the air.

I sought her approval. The worst thing in the world to me was to have her look down on me, which she did a lot. She was always one to condescend. I frequently felt inadequate in her presence. We didn't speak much, but when we did, I made all efforts to conceal my vulgar lifestyle to her. Her ability to evoke shame was unparalleled.

Beyond my sisters, there is a long list of women that have somehow affected me. Some were just sexual encounters; others were friendships that were always more than just a *friendship,* even if they were platonic. There were always women in my life, and I often look back at them as the phases of me—as if the sections of my life are grouped by the woman by my side at the time. The only woman who didn't affect me, or my life, was my mother, who I barely knew throughout my life. She left when I was young. I didn't hear from her in any facet until many years later. But who needs mothers when there are sisters?

# 10

Months had passed since my surgery and engagement, and I had the itch to train again. I knew I wasn't going to be an MMA superstar—or take any punches to the dome—but I wanted to train again. I was a Jiu Jitsu/grappler guy anyway. I wanted to wrestle and submit people and get in shape and lose the extra 15lb swelling up around my midsection.

When I walked into Arizona Combat Sports, as always, I received a warm welcome. When I mentioned that I wanted to train, everyone in earshot fell silent.

"Are you sure?" Trevor Lally asked.

"Yeah. The doctors say I'm okay to go back to normal activity. As long as nobody starts punching me in the face, I think I'll be fine."

My friend, Curt, met me at the gym to train with. He was a nurse at a local hospital, and crazier than Kurt Cobain himself. Curt once spent a month-long stint tripping on 'Shrooms. He'd purchase the psychedelic fungus by the pound, and then grind them up into a powder which he'd then encapsulate in 500mg capsules. That way he knew exactly how much he was taking—not to mention the ease-of-use factor that came along with carrying around capsules that looked like vitamins. It also made them easier to consume while at work, in the Emergency Room. Yes, you heard that correctly. He was tripping while saving lives—hopefully most of them were saved, that is. This is the same guy that showed up to train one day, and after I noticed he was a little sluggish, he pulled up his shirt and exposed the numerous fentanyl patches stuck to his back. When I asked him what he was thinking, he responded, "Just to try it out."

Curt was happy that I was going to attempt a training session. He wasn't as worried about my brain aneurysm as I had been. Not now, not when I was diagnosed. It was his hospital that Steve drove me to upon learning from Dana White about my brain aneurysm.

"Whoa, you got fat," Curt blurted out upon seeing me. "I don't think I've ever seen you this fluffy before. What are you weighing?"

"One-seventy-six," I replied as I grabbed my stomach and love handles.

Now, let me clarify. I know 176-lbs would not be considered fat by most, and it was only about five to ten pounds more than what I weighed before my surgery, but it's how the weight distributes on me that led Curt to bust my balls. See, when I stop working out, at first it's not that noticeable, but then any muscle mass I have atrophies and then is replaced by fat. I don't look fat-fat; I look skinny fat—like Mr. Burns from the Simpsons. Soft. Gangly. Unathletic. And the love handles pop out and I grow a "fupa."

"This is going to suck," I said. "I haven't worked out in almost two years."

"Oh, no. You'll be fine. Like riding a bike."

We started jogging around the mats. My legs clunked while my insides jostled around. If I had ever had any grace while exercising, which I'm not sure I have, it was absent on that day while I plodded around the mats. I started to sweat. It felt good. I rolled my shoulders out and stretched my legs.

"I don't think I'm going to get much warmer," I said. "Let's get this going." I was reluctant, but excited. I could taste the adrenaline in my mouth. It wasn't fight adrenaline, though. It was a mixture of "I'm back" and "I hope I don't die".

Curt started on his back in his guard. I stood in front of him and tried to slide by his legs. He kicked me away. My fingers and hips and legs had butter on them. I slipped around like a drunkard on ice. My lack of grace followed me to Curt's guard. I repeated my attempts. He thwarted them one after the other.

He swept me to my back and began passing my guard. He was heavy. My lungs burned. My hands and forearms swelled with blood and lactic acid. I couldn't grip. He pinned me down—his shoulder in my jaw, driving my face away from him. I made one last ditch attempt to regain my guard. He was a cat and leapt on my back with ease. He morphed into a snake, an anaconda, as his arms wrapped around my neck. They moved slowly, without surprise, as if to say, "I'm going to do this now, and there's nothing you can do to stop me." His arm slithered under my neck, to my shoulder. His other arm wrapped around the back of my neck. His slow, deliberate anaconda squeeze was sucking the fight out of me. The life out of me. The blood out of my brain as it constricted my carotid artery, shutting off the supply of blood from my heart to my head. I tapped.

"That was horrible," I said. I laid on the mat in a puddle of my own sweat. Curt sat waiting for me. "I'm good," I assured myself more than him, and we went back at it.

After thirty minutes of rolling/wrestling, my head hurt began to pound and my stomach spun with nausea.

"I'm done," I said, as I sat against a far wall. Curt grabbed others in the room to roll with, while I sat from the rest of the training and checked my pulse. I pushed my fingers against the bulging veins protruding away from my temples. *Is this right? Should I feel this bad? Is the headache from the surgery?*

"How you feeling, man?" Curt said, startling me as he approached.

"Um, okay. I have a really bad headache, though. You don't think that could be my aneurysm, do you?" I asked. I'd known him for so long at that point, and had asked him about a million medical related questions—most of which he assured me were all in my head and a product of my hypochondriasis.

"Naw, dude. That's just you being out of shape. Those coils and stents are solid, man. If your doctor gave you the go-ahead to start wrestling again, you're fine."

I'm not sure his words helped assuage my fears, but after the veins bulging out of my head receded back, my stomach calmed, and my pulse slowed, and with them, my fears slipped back into my subconscious.

\* \* \*

I kept training. I kept getting into my car after each training session convinced my head was going to explode. I was at the gym more and more and started getting my skills and endurance back. I even had quite a few people ask take private lessons with me, all of which I happily agreed to. Each person was paying me a minimum of $60 an hour and I began to make almost as much in MMA privates as I was making at Vanguard.

Not only did I catch the eye of the rich patrons of the gym, but I also started helping the pro fighters more with their MMA training—especially the submission game, my specialty. So, when Jamie Varner got the call to fight in the UFC against the tough Hermes Franca, Jamie asked me to train with him regularly to help him prepare for Franca's crafty ground game.

When I arrived in Las Vegas, for the fight scheduled for August 6, 2006, I was giddy with excitement. Jamie had cut an ungodly amount of weight over the few days prior to weigh-ins, but seemed in pretty good spirits. I think his total weight loss was 25-lb starting on the previous Monday; it was now Friday.

I'd never been to a live UFC fight, and to be walking around backstage in and out of whatever area I wanted was a special kind of feeling. It was bittersweet, though. I knew that was where I should have been. I knew I should have been in the UFC. I should have been backstage the day of weigh-ins with the rest of the fighters getting ready for the following fight day, but I was currently in the wrong capacity. I was supposed to be sitting where Jamie was. I was supposed to be cutting weight and getting ready for a televised fight with another trained pugilist. As Trevor Lally and Jamie went backstage to wait in line, I sat in a row of bleachers with some other fighters and corner men and waited, looking at the production, the spectacle of the UFC.

Looking around at the spectators, with their cameras flashing and as they clamored around any fighter with a name, I understood the excitement by all. I was watching the stage when I heard a deep voice closely behind my left ear.

"I read that book. It was really good."

I turned around. It was Forrest Griffin. He and I spent a few days hanging out while I was in Athens, Georgia, getting ready to fight Melvin Guillard. He was referring to *The Sea Wolf,* by Jack London—a book I recommend. We chatted for a while, and I somehow felt a little validated, that he remembered me and how well he remembered the details of a few conversations years prior.

*  *  *

## November 2004:

I had just lost a decision in Hawaii to Kaynan Kaku, a BJ Penn trained fighter a few months prior and was looking for another fight when my manager called me.

"You want to fight Melvin Guillard November 20th? He's a wrestler out of Louisiana," Alex, my manager, said.

I knew exactly who he was. I'd just been watching random fights on the internet and came across his fight with Laverne Clarke, a tough fighter out of the Midwest that usually fought at 170-lbs. Guillard was a state champion wrestler and a good kickboxer. He'd recently annihilated a decent BJJ black belt a few months earlier, and I remember thinking, "That is one guy I do not want to fight!"

"What's the pay," I asked?

"Eight hundred dollars. He'll throw in an extra four hundred if you want to go alone without a corner man. The flight money will go to you. I manage a couple of guys out of there that said they'd corner you. You can fly in a few days early and stay with them."

"Sounds good," I said.

I told Trevor what I was doing and he advised me against it. Melvin was a tough fighter, and I had torn cartilage between my ribs. I called my friend Cade and asked him what he thought.

"I don't think that's a good fight for you. He's tough and it's short notice and you got a bum rib. I wouldn't do it."

I didn't listen to anyone. I was in need of cash and I wanted to fight. It annoyed me that Trevor and the other trainers at the gym didn't give me the time and respect I thought I deserved, but I also didn't take their knowledge or advice for much.

When I got to Athens, Georgia, Rory Singer picked me up from the airport. He still had to work for a few days leading up to the fight, so he had Forrest Griffin take me around the city and keep me occupied. Forrest had just finished filming the first season of *The Ultimate Fighter,* but the show hadn't started airing yet. We drove around, stopped by the beautiful college campus, drank coffee, and talked about Leonard Cohen and Modest Mouse, and our favorite music and books.

After a couple of days in Athens, it was time to weigh in. I drove with Rory to Atlanta, where the fight was held and where I'd find my hotel room. Melvin wasn't able to arrive at the weigh-ins on Friday. He was still in Louisiana. The promoter told me he'd weigh-in on Saturday, the day of the fight, which was more than fine with me. Cutting weight sucks, but at least we get 24 hours to recover before fight time. Melvin was going to cut the weight the day of the fight, and try to recover before fight time. Insane to me, but I was happy that it was going to work out that way.

In the morning, I was called downstairs to watch Melvin weigh-in. He weighed-in at 157-lb.

"He's only two pounds over. Is that good?"

"No," I said. "He's gotta lose the weight."

Melvin said nothing and put is sauna suit back on and left the room. An hour later I went back to check his weight. The scale read 156.5.

"He's only a half-pound over. You gotta take that, right?"

"Keep running. I'll see you guys again when he's a half pound lighter."

I didn't want to give Melvin any opportunities to feel great and win that fight. He did come in at 156 on the dot an hour later—within the one-pound weight allowance commissions generally give to fighters in a non-title bout.

The fight took place in a ring, and looking back, the talent in there at the time amazes. Melvin became a UFC fighter. Rory became a UFC fighter. Forrest became the first *Ultimate Fighter* winner and a UFC champ. Hell, even the ref, Jason Miller, eventually became a UFC fighter and TV host.

When the bell rang, I threw a hook and shot in for the takedown. Melvin defended and threw us both in the air. When we landed, I pounced on his back. He grabbed my neck and pulled me into him, folding my torso in half. My rib screamed in pain. I slid down to the canvas and onto my back. Melvin was on top of me. I kicked him off and shot in for a leg.

He grabbed my neck and jumped to his back, hoping to choke me with a guillotine. I popped my head out and threw some punches at him. He kicked me off and stood back to his feet. We clinched against the ropes.

He kneed me in the midsection. Again, my rib cried out, "No more!" I tripped him to the ground, but he exploded and reversed me.

I threw my legs up over his neck and into a triangle choke. He rolled and flailed, but my legs were too tight. He tapped. I leapt up and Rory, and his brother Adam and Forrest ran into the ring.

I'd won.

I'd beaten a legitimately formidable opponent. I'd beaten a guy with a 16-3 record.

\* \* \*

Jamie's fight day had come, and I pummeled with him in between rounds of mitt-work with Trevor. He didn't exude confidence like he normally did. His movements were strong, powerful, but I didn't see a killer in his eyes.

"How do you feel?" I asked. "Ready?"

"I feel good. Just my legs feel a little weak. A little wobbly."

*That's not good. His nerves got him. He's done.* I thought. Wobbly legs are the tell-tale sign of nerves and adrenaline taking over. Once that happens, it's almost always too late. The mind needs to be oblivious to loss. A much less skilled fighter without doubt in his mind is way more dangerous than a skilled fighter that's aware he can lose. Blissful naivety is good for a fighter—so is unabashed arrogance or, sometimes even stupidity. Doubt though? Nope. Doubt's a career killer. Doubt is the fastest way to a loss there is. Doubt is focusing on the uncontrollable. What if I get knocked out? What if I get embarrassed? What if my opponent is strong or fast or I get tired? Doubt causes anxiety's physical manifestation, and the dreaded adrenaline dump.

Doubt rears its head in all facets of our lives: what if I fail the test? What if I stutter during my speech? What if I bomb the job interview? But we can't focus on those things. We can only focus on what we can control. Did I study hard? Did I practice the speech again and again? Am I well qualified for the job? If we focus on what we can control, we take the power out of the unknown, and back into ourselves. We can only control what we can control.

Jamie jumped up and down a few times in hopes of alleviating the weakness. He was focusing on all of the things he couldn't control: the crowd, his opponent, the opportunity, and the big stage. Shortly after our conversation, it was time to fight.

He fought well, but he fought scared. A couple of times he was reversed and put on the mat or too close to the fence and he turned his back to

Rich was a short, stocky man with a grumbling voice. He graveled his way through sentences—often incomprehensible, but eventually he'd garble out enough syllables to get his point across. He and I drank bottle after bottle of Jack Daniels for hours on end, on more nights than I could count, since I'd given up abstaining. We laughed and yelled out nonsensicals at one another until the dawn hovered over us. I was glad to learn he'd be fighting in Hawaii with Edwin, Kauai, and me.

*Rumble on the Rock,* a fight promotion out of Hawaii asked the four of us to fight on the card after Joe Riggs, our training partner, fought for them in a losing battle against the large-headed Hawaiian brute, Wesley "Cabbage" Coreirra. The promotion was in need of some other mainlanders to pit against local Hawaiians for their second card and somehow Roland got the call. This was my first "real" fight. When I say "real" I mean, it was the first fight I would actually be paid more than $35 for. It was the first fight I would have to travel for. And it was by far the toughest opponent I'd faced at that point in my career.

Kauai, who is named after the Hawaiian island, was not as excited to be going-to-freaking-Hawaii! Rich was excited, but he'd been to Hawaii before, among the many other fantastical lands he'd jet-setted to, throughout his life. Edwin and I were young, though. We had never been anywhere or done anything. Hawaii was our coming of age. When we left Phoenix Sky Harbor airport we were two 19-year-old kids. When we landed in Hilo, HI, we were not necessarily men, but we were no longer children either.

My short stint with Jonelle was coming to an end. Her parents were pressuring her to go back to the church, so we stopped seeing each other. If you're going to get dumped for someone it may as well be God. It was a short relationship, but it opened my eyes to what was out in the world. When I met her I was young and inexperienced. I hadn't traveled or done anything of note. My relationships had all been high-schoolish, but she introduced me to life as an adult. I was unhappy with the waning of our relationship, but hearing that I would be traveling to a paradise island to fight, assuaged my emotions. Jonelle called me to wish me good luck after my arrival in Hilo, but I had already started to move on to a new love: Hawaii.

Roland, Rich, Edwin, Kauai and myself deplaned. When we got to baggage claim there were people holding signs with our names on them like we'd seen in the movies. We grabbed our bags and giddily jumped into a long white passenger van where a man with the deepest demon voice said, "Hey guys, I'm Alex. I'm the announcer for the show. Remember, the legal age is 16 here."

"Legal age? For drinking?" I asked.

"For sex!"

The group of hoales (what Hawaiians call whites) all looked at one another in amazement.

Edwin and I grinned. We may as well have been in a different country. The air was humid and warm. The airport was open-air, and the second we exited the plane we could feel the breeze roll off of the ocean. The people were all brown and talked differently—we could barely understand them and wondered if they were speaking English or some language we were unfamiliar with. We were on an island in the middle of the Pacific to fight and we were going to get paid for it.

Our hotel was only a few minutes from the Hilo airport and sat right on the ocean. Edwin and I roomed together. We slid the hotel key into the lock, and when the door clicked and a green light flicked at us, we pushed it open and threw our bags on the bed. There were, thankfully, two beds and a television that we barely touched during our stay. In the bathroom, were the standard soaps and lotions one expects to see at a mid-level vacation hotel and, fortunately, a window air conditioning unit. There was nothing exceptional about it, but what it represented was that we had made a move in life. We had taken a step up the next rung on the ladder, and we both knew it.

As a child, I never envisioned myself working. Never once. Working in an office or cubicle on a computer never once crossed my mind. I knew I didn't want to be any type of laborer—I was way too good for that. The future didn't exist. Every now and again, if people asked, I'd try to picture what life would be like for me. There was literally nothing. A blank picture. A background of a field or city or ocean with no foreground. No subject. No me. I always thought that I'd be dead at thirty-five, anyway. It wasn't that I was suicidal or even reckless enough to warrant a death so young, it's just that I couldn't actually visualize something beyond that. After thirty, you're old, I thought. I didn't want to be old. I—me—the most incredible person in the world couldn't get old. I was Dorian Gray without the spell. Anytime I did think of the future, thoughts of grandeur seeped in. Maybe I'd be the President, or a Navy SEAL, or a CIA assassin, or the ruler of the world. Getting to Hawaii was one step toward that maniacal delusion, but one step further from reality.

Edwin was larger than me and had been fighting for a few years before I came to Brausa. He was Roland's crown jewel, and in the eyes of our small MMA world at the time, he was the best fighter of any of us. He was 6' 1" and weighed around two hundred and ten pounds and fought at the light-heavyweight division. His bones were huge. He had wrists the size of my ankles, and ankles the size of my thighs. His hair was always dyed platinum blonde, and I barely ever witnessed a dark root. Both front teeth were chipped. He dropped out of high school and decided to pursue fighting full time when he was 17. Edwin grew up in a poor household like I had, but for some reason, I never related to him. I should have. I would have if we had met years earlier, but I had grown up. I grew a purpose somewhere along the line. He and I always looked and spoke to one another like strangers. I always worried that if he didn't make it at fighting, he wouldn't make it in life. I was uneasy around him. Not like I worried about him stabbing me in the gut with a number two pencil or anything, but more that we didn't have anything in common.

We arrived in Hilo, Hawaii, on Wednesday, and our fight wasn't until Saturday. Friday would be for weight cutting, but the rest of Wednesday and all of Thursday would be ours to do with as we chose.

Rich was somewhere with Roland, so Kauai, Edwin, and I went for a walk into town. I had built my professional record to 4-1 and was feeling confident of my abilities to get into a cage with another human with the sole purpose of harming him. After my initial 1-1 record in my first two bouts I went on a three fight win streak. There was Daniel De Souza, a Brazilian with a black belt in Jiu Jitsu, whom I put a solid beating on before he quit with a shoulder injury in the second round. Then there was Joe Vigil, the same fellow that had bested me as an amateur in the most disgusting display of fights the world had seen. I submitted him with a Kimura (shoulder lock) a minute and a half into the first round.

The fourth win of my career came by most spectacular fashion, as I beat the life and death out of a good gentleman from California named Randy Spence. I kicked his leg so many times it was purple-- almost black with bruising-- but in the third round, with only seconds left, I jumped into a triangle choke and forced him to tap. That was at the Dodge Theatre in Phoenix, in front of the largest crowd I had fought in front of and where I met Angie Diercks, the next lady in my life. With my win over Randy, I got the nod from Roland to go to Hawaii with the rest of the crew.

As Edwin, Kauai, and I walked down the streets of Hilo Hawaii, we took pictures while standing on rocks in the water, swung from trees, and ran in the shallow water of an inlet cove until Kauai told us that was where the sharks came to birth their young to keep them from predators, and get them used to swimming before they go into deep, rough waters. Edwin and I quickly exited the cove and kept our feet on un-sharked territory after that. The next day, Rich's father came to the island to watch the fight and we drove around the island. Roland bought one of those cheesy hats woven out of some kind of plant life. He looked ridiculous –understatement -- but we didn't have the heart to tell him. When we got back to the hotel later that night, we ate a small meal and left Roland downstairs in the weight room where he was hitting on a housekeeper. Our night ended early. We had to make weight the next day. Kauai didn't have to lose weight. One of the perks of fighting as a heavyweight is the lack of dieting; probably to make up for the discomfort and minimal legroom on airplanes. Edwin and Rich had to lose about five pounds each; and I had to lose about 12.

I woke early. The sun hadn't come through our window yet, but we were operating on Arizona time, which, depending on the time of year can vary from three to four hours difference. Arizona doesn't believe in daylight savings. Or gun laws. I waited for Edwin to wake up, but he just laid on his bed, lifeless, for longer than my anxiety-to-start-my-weight-cut could handle. I grabbed a room key, and scurried off to the gym with my sweats and sauna suit by myself. With twelve pounds to lose, I didn't have time to waste.

The gym was small, consisting of a few treadmills and a weight machine, but it also had a sauna—my preferred method for weight loss. I pulled the top of my sauna suit—plasticky-nylon sweatshirts and pants to heat your body up to temperatures it is not meant to sustain—over my head and onto my body, covering my sweatshirt. Then I pulled another sweatshirt over the plastic, suffocating material. I did the same with the pants—pulling them over my sweatpants, and then pulling sweats above the nylon. The room was empty, but it was bright and brought my spirits up with the view outside where I could see the ocean crash onto the black boulders. There were also children playing with their parents on the lawn of the hotel in the warm sticky air.

I stared at the waves as I turned the treadmill onto six miles per hour to get my heart rate up. Before I took my first step I could already feel the drops of sweat percolating through my skin and into the cotton shirt below the sauna suit.

Sauna suits are vice grips on your lungs. Almost immediately after putting one on you will feel like shit. After a few minutes of running you feel like your lungs are going to burst and you can't get any oxygen to your heart. You think you're drowning in your own body. If worn too long, the sauna suit is life threatening.

I kept jogging for over an hour at various speeds to maintain the sweat I had. After the first thirty minutes, I took the sweatshirt I had under the suit off. It was too wet, which can actually cool your body, antithetical to weight loss.

The waves splashing onto the black rocks were no longer soothing and became torturous. I wanted to jump in the cool water and save my soul from scalding. I was a man standing in Hades, parched, while the water rose just below my fingertips, which held a cup to collect my saving liquid. I wanted to drink from the ocean and see if the salt truly would take my life. I wanted water. I needed water.

The hell was just beginning. I hadn't even sat in the sauna yet, and I was already losing my focus. My feet were tired on the first thousand steps up Everest, and I hadn't even found my way to base camp.

I jumped off of the treadmill, which had puddles of sweat dripping down the face of the LCD screen and even more down the sides of its base. I removed my suit and top layer of sweat pants leaving nothing on but my soaked boxer brief underwear. The coolness of the air sang to my skin like a Baptist church choir on a hot, muggy day in southern Mississippi. I laid on a workout bench for a few minutes before I admonished myself for "being a pussy." I put my plastics back on and sat in the sauna where the temperature read 180 degrees. Within moments, beads of ocean water seeped from my pores. As the moisture formed beads on my head it formed little creeks and rivers that flowed down the sides of my face and entered the waterfall from my chin to the floor. I frequently flicked my pruning hand through my hair and sent a spray of the moisture to the wooden floor or walls of my torture chamber. I went in for twenty minutes and out for ten minutes until I had reached an hour in total time in the sauna before I checked my weight.

As I got out of the sauna, Rich, Kauai, Edwin, and Roland walked in. Roland looked like he'd been cutting weight with me for twenty-eight hours.

"What's up, Franco?" Edwin yelled rhetorically, with a smile on his face. "How much ya got to lose?"

"I don't know yet. I'm about to check right now."

"You're sweaty as shit. You're pretty damn close. Well, at least you look better than Roland," he said, then laughed as he looked at the broken man, our trainer, who sat on the floor with his face down.

"He banged one of the housekeepers last night, you little white bitch!" Kauai yelled.

I was pulling the last of my sweats off when Roland said, "Franco, she rode me like a train. Like a caboose. Chugga-chugga, chugga-chugga, choo-choo." Then he laid down on the gym floor and covered his eyes with his arm.

I stood on the scale and moved the little weights back and forth until the lever of the scale suspended in the air signaling my exact weight.

"Fuck, I still have six more pounds," I said.

"Ah, shit, that'll be easy, Santino," Rich said. He was the only one of the group that used my proper name.

I put my plastics back on and in the heat I went like a fireman into a blazing house. I forced myself into the blaze with nothing to protect me but my will. My body was defeated; the stink of burned hair hit my nostrils before I got to the flames. As I forged on, my skin started to melt away, exposing the red fleshy fibers of my muscles. The black smoke masked the red and orange waves of the incinerator, as my muscles turned black and burned away like a T-bone left on the grill for too long. Eventually, I was nothing but a skeleton moving through a burning building looking for survivors. But my body was not needed. It could not help me. The only thing that could help me was my mind—if I could keep it calm enough to realize that I wasn't going to die, and that if I fainted, someone would drag me out of the heat and resuscitate me.

It may sound excessive, but the weight cut is by far the hardest part of the fight preparation. It's not uncommon for people to end up in the hospital after a poorly planned weight cut, and many feel they are going to die during the process—not metaphorically, or hyperbolically, but literally die. Every so often someone actually does die. More often than not, though, they just find themselves in the hospital with damaged kidneys to match the damaged pride of not making weight, which usually means a cancelled bout as well.

I opened my eyes and looked back at the ocean and yearned for a giant tsunami to crash down on me, the gym, the sauna—everything. To absorb me. To become me. Maybe when it hit, I would just dissolve into molecules and become the sea, I thought. I looked out and saw Kauai drinking from a water bottle. He pulled it from his mouth and poured the rest of it onto the floor while looking at me with a smile on his face. I looked down silently.

*Water, water everywhere, and all the boards did shrink. Water, water everywhere, nor any drop to drink.*

My leg started to bounce, almost uncontrollably. I clenched my jaw as I shook my head. The air was hot and it was hard to get it into my lungs. I started to break. Mentally, I was losing the fight. I hadn't even stepped in the cage yet, hadn't even fought my first fight outside of Arizona, and I was breaking. My mind raced and swirled around in the waves that were staring at me and I felt the panic approaching. It started to climb up the base of my spine like pin pricks on its way up to my brain. It was over. I knew it. Then, I looked back outside and saw the kids playing again. There was a little boy, maybe four or five, chasing his older sister.

The boy made me think of my own sisters. When I was young, I chased them around yelling, "Let's play a game. Any game. You name it, I'll play it." Rarely did that work, but I hated being alone and I would rather have them shooing me away than actually be away, alone.

Before my parents divorced, my sisters and I played in a small clearing in the woods next to our brown house in Theresa, during the summers. To get there we had to walk up a hill, through twenty or so yards of trees, and then we saw a number of tree stumps, coated with sawdust. We sat at our stumps, collecting sawdust in our buckets, and pretended it was coffee and tea. We sat out there, peacefully. Happy. We didn't know there was a divorce looming. We didn't know anything but dirt and rhubarb and sawdust and imaginary friends. The day after my father went to jail for pulling out the gun, I played by the stumps for as long as I could. The sawdust was plentiful. It felt cool as I picked it up in my hands and let it fall between my fingers. I was safe on the tree stumps with the finely ground dust of the fallen trees. After what seemed like hours, my sisters joined me. Chea and Adrianna put their arms around me—hugging me tightly—and Chea said, "Don't worry. It's going to be okay, Tino."

I'm not sure whether it was or wasn't okay, but I certainly believed them at the time. The stump, and tiny pieces of chipped trees fell out through my fingers while my sisters' arms were wrapped around me, is a memory I return to for solace and strength.

The sawdust kept me out of the flames of the sauna just long enough for the panic to subside. I continued to lie in a puddle of my own life, as it slowly leaked out of my body.

\* \* \*

Drained of water, and annoyed, I stood on the scale as Alexander Oxendine yelled out, "Santino DeFranco weighs in at one hundred and fifty-four pounds!"

My opponent, Jamal Perkins, a local favorite with a perfect-undefeated record of eight wins and zero losses, and I faced one another after we both made weight. I clenched my jaw and stared down at the brown man. He was shorter than me but more muscular.

"Oh boy, Franco, you looked pissed. Right, guys? Franco's a killer. You see that look in his eyes?" Roland joked to the rest of our group as I pulled my clothes on.

I grabbed a large bottle of water and started drinking it the moment my pants were over my legs. I drank the thirty-two-ounce bottle in under a minute. Within moments of finishing it, I started to sweat—a common occurrence after the first drink of water following a weight cut.

I continued to drink and eat everything I could for the entirety of the evening, and when I went to bed, I almost felt like a human.

We arrived at the arena the next day around five in the evening. It was an old airplane hangar that had been converted into an open-air venue. The air was full of thick, heavy moisture that was hard to breathe. Once inside the hanger, we navigated through the murky air, making our way to the far back, where our "locker rooms" were going to be. Our warm-up area was as open as the hangar without so much as a curtain dividing the opponents. Edwin, Rich, and I went to the cage to scope out our battlefield and eye the locals and the venue.

The worst part of fight night is always the wait. I can only imagine how a soldier feels right before battle, especially centuries ago when the two sides stood waiting for battle only hundreds of yards from each other. As fighters we face one trillionth of the danger that they face, and the fear is barely controllable.

The fight program stated the show would start at 7:30 p.m.; however, in the history of fights, not a single one has ever been started at the advertised time. The fights in Hilo, Hawaii, that night didn't start until well after 8 p.m. We sat there, warming up with each other, and helping Shannon Ritch warm up, too, as he had booked our fights for us, but wasn't really part of us. He had MMA legend Don Fry in his corner, but as Don was more concerned with a vacation and sun tanning than helping Shannon, we allowed the "most hated man in MMA" to come over to our team for a bit.

After warming up, we sat on the floor, realizing we would still have a long time before any of our fights. I was the first fight out of our group, but I was still seventh in the overall line up. We were not going anywhere anytime soon. We talked to pass the time. We listened to music. We paced back and forth (a lot). We shadowboxed. We paced some more. We laid down on the dirt floor, closed our eyes, and ran through our fights in our minds. We snuck glimpses of the previous fights. We repeated everything multiple times. We worried. We waited.

Finally, it was time for me to warm up.

I ran wind sprints in the parking lot to get my legs warm then went inside to hit mitts with Roland, who had no clue how to hold them—he was a grappler and knew little about striking. I shadowboxed and wrestled with Rich Moss to get ready to go out to the cage. The butterflies that fluttered in my stomach in unison made me hopeful and confident to wage battle. Then, just as quickly, they raged war on my stomach. They brought self-doubt and uncertainty. I fought back though. Nerves before a fight, nerves before any exciting endeavor, are the same nerves we get when climbing a steep rollercoaster. On the way up, we look around. We look down. We look at the rollercoaster and think of the person who put that bolt there and this lever here. We analyze. We rationalize with ourselves. *Of course it's going to be fine. People do this all the time.* But emotion doesn't give a shit about rationale and we become nervous. We become anxious. But there's nothing we can do at this point. The rollercoaster is at the top. It is going to drop, whether we want it to or not—whether we like it or not. And it does drop. And when it does we have two options: close our eyes in fear and wait for it to end; or open our eyes, put our hands up and scream in excitement.

The fight before mine ended and a white guy with a Pidgeon accent came back to me to tell me I was up. I walked to the ramp entrance to the cage and waited for my music to play. Eminem was rocking the airwaves of entrance music in the MMA scene at the time, but I swam against the current and came out to Nelly's *I am number one*. It took the DJ a few moments to get it started, and then the chorus takes another minute before it gets going. I wanted to come out to the words, "I am number one, no matter if you like it, until you sit down and write it," but Roland was pushing me.

"Franco, you gotta go. Come on. They're waiting for you."

I took a step then stopped.

"They can wait," I said as I stood at the top of the ramp, looking down at the cage and crowd. Shadowboxing while my music got ramped up to the point where I was ready. The chorus came and I took a step. Most of the other fighters that night nearly ran to the cage. I took my time and shadowboxed for the crowd. I slapped the hands of spectators; I held my hands in the air to the sound of boos from the locals. Jamal was already in the cage waiting for me. It's funny, I waited all day to have my name called, but when it finally was, I took my sweet-ass time getting there. I played the crowd and loved every second of it. There was smoke behind me and lights in front of me. I was happy. I climbed in the cage and bounced around. Jamal Perkins stood on the other side looking at me with forceful eyes. I was entertaining, I was playing the crowd, but he was only there for business. There was nothing flashy about him or his entrance—no pomp and circumstance. He was there to fight, and only that.

We came to the center of the cage and exchanged furrowed scowls. The ref instructed us to touch gloves. Our hands met and we went to our corners to wait for the opening bell. The time for waiting, and flights, and weight cuts, and oceans, and engaging the crowd, and roads to greatness, and everything else was locked out of the cage. Jamal and the referee were the only ones in there with me.

*Ding. Ding.*

He came at me fast. He was a southpaw, which threw me off, as I had never fought a left-hander before. He shot in to take me to the ground, but I shrugged him off. *Little fucker's fast.* He sprang back to his feet and I threw a knee to his head, which missed, causing me to fall backwards to the ground. *Shit. Grab his head and arm so he can't elbow you. Scoot your hips out. Wrist control. Slide your leg over his neck. Grab your ankle.* I had my legs wrapped around his head and arm, setting up a triangle choke. He lifted me in the air like we were in the middle of a clean-and-jerk weightlifting competition. *Oh shit! I'm going up. Now I'm going down. Tuck your head.* SLAM. We hit the canvas hard, but I held my legs tight around him, and the force actually pushed him further in the chokehold. *Grab his head. Squeeze.* His hand motioned to quit. He tapped out.

I didn't jump up with elation after the win. I popped up to my feet and paraded around the cage with my hands in the air. I bowed to the audience with a sense of confidence. I won my first *real* fight. It was a different country to me. My career had just begun. The second Jamal tapped out I knew I could fight. I knew I could fight for a living. And, I knew I could fight at a high level. Jamal wasn't a "name" opponent, but beating him let me know I was capable of something more than winning in the local scene. I wasn't a big fish in a big pond, but I knew if I ate enough, and was careful, I would grow. I would grow to something worthy of the ocean. I would grow into something beyond job titles and cubicles and degrees. I would grow into something bigger than those—greater than those. Wouldn't I?

After my fight, the others were up.

Rich went out to fight next, and after an illegal head-butt, the fight was called a no contest. Edwin beat his guy easily, and Kauai knocked out his opponent who had a big name and was supposed to be on his way to the big show, using Kauai as a tune up fight or stepping stone. And, Roland...well, he was drunk before we left the arena.

# 12

After Kindal's father agreed to lend me the money, I called Rich and told him, "Let's do it!"

I put in my notice at Vanguard and felt liberated. I'd never fight again, but at least I could instill my knowledge into the next generation of fighters and be around the sport I loved and that had given me so much. I'd set up a training schedule at Edwin's gym, West Coast MMA, where I would be teaching for two weeks while Edwin was away training for a fight. That would give the students a few weeks to get to know me, and when it was announced that I would be taking over as head trainer, the transition should be a lot smoother. Edwin hadn't built up a huge stable of students, but there were enough to cover rent for the small strip mall space and utilities—maybe 25 students total.

I was having a blast teaching Edwin's students and they seemed to be very thankful of my teaching style as well. Students would regularly come up to me after class thanking me and telling me they were learning a lot. After the two-week trial, Rich handed Edwin the check on a Friday, and the gym was ours. Monday was a fresh start, and the beginning of a new chapter. I'd quit Vanguard, the students I was training at Arizona Combat Sports were going to continue training with me at my new location, and I was back in MMA. I was free. For the first time in a long time, optimistic about my future. I saw myself as a big-name trainer in the coming years.

Monday, I trained with one of my private-lesson students, Tom Gavrilos, an awkward, social media-obsessed guy who had made money buying and selling houses during the height of the housing boom. He constantly boasted about his *MySpace* followers, ranging in the hundreds of thousands. After our training session had ended, I waited at the desk for the students to show up for the 4pm MMA class. As the minutes wound down, I cleaned the mats, cleaned the bathroom and restocked the paper towels and toilet paper, I organized my desk with anticipation.

To my surprise, everyone was late. The clock read 4:25pm. I began to worry. 5 o'clock came and went. Nobody showed up. 6 o'clock came. Still nobody. At 8 o'clock I locked the doors. Not a single human stepped through the doors. This process repeated Tuesday, Wednesday, Thursday and Friday. Friday I locked the doors to a dream that had turned into a nightmare. *What the hell happened? Did the students not like me? Damn. I just threw away my career at Vanguard for this. For this?! I made a big mistake.*

Months later I'd find out that Edwin had called every student he ever had after Rich had given him that check and told each of them that he'd moved locations. Not that I'd bought the gym. Not that he wouldn't be training them anymore. But that he'd moved. West Coast MMA had moved to a new location and had changed their name.

I'd been bamboozled. A career in finance and, more importantly, the paychecks that accompany that career, were gone, replaced by a non-existent business, a leased space with a few mats in it and a new name.

If I'd embarked on it alone, I'd have given up right there. Thankfully, I hadn't. Rich busted his ass calling every person he knew in the MMA and Judo world, bringing us our first paying students within a few weeks. He also footed the bill for rent and utilities for the first three months. As the days and weeks passed, I wondered what was to come of my illustrious training career. It certainly hadn't started out the way I anticipated.

Then, one day in November, an old training partner brought an aspiring fighter to my gym named Seth Baczynski. He was a tall, lanky, uncoordinated man. We started training and I easily submitted him within a minute, then again, and again. When the timer finally rung, ending our round together he was in disbelief.

"Let's go again," Seth said.

"Okay."

Again, I submitted him.

"Again," Seth said.

And again, I submitted him.

This pattern continued for over a half an hour until I was thoroughly exhausted.

"Come on, man, you got to give me one more chance."

"Not a chance. I'm so tired I can't move. I'm done. Come back tomorrow and I'll give you another chance," I joked.

And he did. He came back again and again and again. He was by no means the most athletic human I'd ever met, but he had an iron lung, endurance for days, and a toughness that a bull would envy. Like me, he came from a trailer, and had a really bad upbringing. I could certainly read and write a lot better than him, but he could hit a hell of a lot harder than me and didn't have a brain aneurysm, so there was that. He was tough, had a good chin, and hit like a truck and he was willing to learn. I was more than happy to work with him.

Seth eventually brought over his entire crew of fighters and friends from Brausa, Seth, Danny Martinez, Yaotzin Meza—all eventual UFC vets—came over along with quite a few others creating my stable of fighters almost overnight.

## 13

The faded yellow trailer was almost entirely unnoticeable from the road. The driveway was not paved, just a clearing that led into the wooded area where, off to the left, our trailer sat hidden behind large pines and the occasional maple. The trailer was hidden, just as we were. Hidden from the road. Hidden from our mother. Hidden from the power company and the water company and the phone company. We were hidden from the town and the twentieth century. My sisters and I didn't know we were hidden, though, we just thought we had gone home to the woods where our memories were the fondest.

Before the divorce, we lived in a large brown farmhouse on one hundred acres. We played outside all day long and into the night until the stars and moon shone silver and told us we had to stop dreaming for the day. We stomped our bare feet through the mud and ran to the stream out back where we tied logs together to form rafts that never floated. If they had, the rafts would have taken us down the stream and into the large rivers and into the ocean where our adventures would begin. We ate wild strawberries and raspberries we found while hunting for toads and frogs in the pond behind the stream because the berries in our father's garden never grew. The rhubarb did, though, and we plucked it by the stalk and dipped it in bowls of sugar, then snapped the bittersweet combination into our mouths until our stomachs hurt. Chea, the ladybug lover, made houses and villages for her red friends with black dots, and I followed Adrianna to the ladybug villages and we'd stomp the townspeople out. Chea, though always mad at us for doing so, never retaliated. She just wanted to be left alone with her bugs.

Adrianna was my general, and as a good private, I obeyed every order she barked, until one day she ordered me to dress up in our father's clothes and start his truck, so I could go see my imaginary girlfriend, Sally. The truck's engine roared and the wheels lurched forward before the manual transmission failed me and it died out. Our father came out of the house screaming.

"What the hell are you doing, Tino?"

"I'm going to see Sally," I replied.

"Who the hell is Sally?" he yelled.

"My girlfriend." I couldn't believe he didn't know who Sally was, so I said the words with such contempt, I thought he was going to rupture upon hearing them. He didn't rupture. He actually calmed down and asked, "Where are your sisters?"

"Over here," Chea said, as they reared their faces from behind the corner of the house. Their fear did a lousy job of masking their smirks and they received a verbal lashing. We went back to playing in the mud and angering our father by running through his dilapidated garden.

I had a pair of Superman pajamas that came with a red cape that I wore all day long. I told my sisters I could lift up the house. I don't think they believed me.

"Why don't you do it then?" they'd reply.

"I don't want to. I'm tired right now."

When they weren't looking I'd grab a piece of the siding and pull to the sky with my might. I was convinced it was because I wasn't giving it my all that the house didn't budge, but if I really set my mind to the task it would break from its foundation, leaving me with our living arrangements in my hands, above my head. I knew then, that if I'd really try, I'd be great. I'd be a superhero—if I wasn't one already.

While in full Superman uniform, I jumped from the top of my dresser onto my bed to fly again and again. One day, Adrianna talked me out of jumping from my second story bedroom window, as I wanted to fly away. I didn't know what I was flying away from. I think I wanted to fly toward being a superhero more than I wanted to leave something. I had everything I ever wanted and would have surely returned shortly. She convinced me never to try to jump out of the window again, and to stick with jumping off of the dresser.

I played in my room with my *Thundercats* action hero men when my sisters were at school, and when Chea came home she forced me to learn what she did that day, whether I wanted to or not. I knew how to read, count, add, and subtract before I was four.

It was because of those memories we immediately thought of the trailer as being "home" when we saw the yellow canister sitting there in the woods on part of the land that we owned with the brown house. After the divorce, my father sold the house and five acres with it. He kept the rest, which was where the trailer then sat. As soon as we arrived to the trailer we continued our perpetual play in the woods that we were so familiar with and, once again, the enchanted nights, when the wind blew cool after hot summer days, were ours.

Some things had never been part of our old life at the brown house. We didn't have running water which meant no showers. It also meant we had to go to the bathroom outside, and fetch water from the beaver pond, far into the woods, to drink. In its raw state, the water was un-consumable. We first filtered it through a t-shirt or sheet or other cloth to get the large sediment out. Then we boiled the water on our outside grill, which consisted of a fire and an oven rack to ensure it was healthy enough to drink. The gritty water never won any taste awards, but it served its purpose well, and on the path to the pond we ate raspberries the size of quarters that grew from the bushes. We smelled the large treats well before we ever saw them. Once the smell hit our noses our mouths watered. We knew the berries were near, and the pond was just around the corner.

There was no electricity, but that didn't bother us much. We never really watched TV or played video games, and our father had an old portable TV that he had connected to a car battery. He charged the battery at our neighbor's house on a weekly basis, which allowed him to watch reruns of M.A.S.H. 4077 regularly.

The trailer also lacked heat, which, in the summer, was of no consequence, but during the frigid winters of Upstate New York, near the Canadian border, it was deathly. We did have a kerosene heater which we used to warm the front room, and we all slept there during the winter, as the rest of the trailer was a freezer. One day our father was angry at Adrianna, and sent her to the back of the trailer in the cold. She sat there for hours in the cold trying not scream. When she was finally allowed to rejoin the rest of us, her face was red—beet red. She shook uncontrollably and cried for hours.

I never realized there was anything wrong with any of this. Even as Adrianna cried on the bus-ride home from school one day—it still didn't hit me.

"What's wrong?" I asked.

"Nothing, Tino. Nothing. Leave me alone."

Adrianna then whispered to Chea that a group of kids were making fun of her for smelling. Chea assured her she didn't smell and that it was the just the kerosene from the heater that they smelled.

"We don't smell like kerosene," I thought. "What are they talking about? Why would that be bad anyway?"

I went home not understanding the cruelties of school children and continued my normal course. After that day, Chea and Adrianna didn't climb as many pine trees as I did. I would sit in the trees with sap covering my skin and matted in my hair, smelling the needles and daydreaming about being a superhero, but they refrained from more and more of the things that separated them from the other school children.

We ate mostly spaghetti with oil and garlic powder (or whatever else the church pantry had for people like us) for food along with any fish my father caught from the nearby river. He was a lousy fisherman, so if he caught anything, it was sunfish or perch. The occasional bass would appear on our grill, which I know I should have enjoyed, but never got past the fishy taste. We also scoured the woods and the side of the road for my favorite treat, milkweed—a soft, fluffy weed that when the leaves were plucked, would ooze a white liquid. We'd spend hours collecting the greens on the side of the road, then boil it and add oil, or margarine if it was available, and salt and pepper. It was a favorite for all of us.

As winter neared, our father realized we were going to need extra protection from the wind and snow that would be upon us within a couple of months. He enlisted our services, to cut down trees with him and build an extra room next to the trailer that would give us more living space, and offer some coverage from the angry winter assault. For weeks we hauled logs out of the woods after our father cut them down. We stripped them of their branches then hoisted them up to him on the roof of the trailer as he pounded nails into them. Once finished, the new room was quite large, but used mostly for cooking on the grill. Without a door it offered shelter from the wind and snow, but nothing more. It was as cold as the snow-covered dirt under the pine trees.

Whenever I tell people about my time living in the trailer, they ask, "How did you make it through that?" They look at me with pity. They feel sorry for me. I reciprocate their sentiments. I sometimes feel sorry for others for having an easy life—for having a normal life. I don't wish any human, especially small children, or, God forbid, my own children— to ever live without running water or heat or electricity. But I wouldn't trade the experiences for normalcy. I have a deep understanding of not having things. Of being poor. I understand what it means to have nothing. I understand what it means to look at someone with less than me and not to feel contempt or pity, but to understand that he or she is just in a different place than I am now.

But I also understand that my life could have been so much worse. I could have been raised in similar conditions in Africa or Mexico, where I might not have had the opportunity for upward mobility like I've had in the States. I understand that that mobility is a gift given to me—not something I really earned, but gifted. I was born a white man in the United States of America during the twentieth century. I might not be the most attractive human, but I'm not ugly—I don't have any birth defects or physical deformities or ailments. I'm not Einstein, but I have a relatively functional brain with a functional IQ. Living those years in the trailer with nothing but my sisters and the wilderness taught me that I am lucky. I am fortunate for my experiences and the life I was lucky enough to be born into.

* * *

When I got home from Hawaii, I went straight to my father's. I lived across town with Jed, but my father's house was my home. Wherever he was would always be considered home, plumes of smoke or not.

"How'd you do, Teen?" he asked when I opened the door.

"I won! I beat him in the first round. Fast." I put my arm around his thin shoulder. He sucked on a cigarette with a long ash leaning toward the ground, the ember glaring off of his bifocal glasses. He looked older. It had been a few weeks since I had seen him, but he had aged a decade. He was sixty-one at the time. He looked eighty-five. The entire top row of his teeth had been extracted a few years prior by the dentists at the Veterans Hospital and he'd been fitted for dentures. He rarely wore them, though. He said they didn't fit right and made his mouth hurt. I never cared much for the reason and didn't hide my embarrassment of his dental hygiene. When we ate at restaurants he always made a habit of asking if the food was soft. "Are the vegetables well done? I don't have any teeth in the upper part of my mouth, so it's hard for me to chew?" he'd say as he showed them his mouth and I avoided eye contact with the server.

As the burning cigarette roared a fire red, I noticed his eyes were foggier than usual and his eyelids were sagging. His bulbous Italian nose was starting to fall toward the table continuously, but he'd catch himself and jerk his head and neck back upright.

"Dad, are you okay? Did you take too much meds? You don't look well."

"I'm good, Teen. The doctor made some changes to my pills since I haven't been sleeping good," he said then he picked up a bottle from his medicine basket. "He has me taking three of these a day." The bottle read *Carisoprodol* (generic for *Soma.)* He grabbed another bottle. "He wants me taking two of these a day." The bottle read *Diazepam* (generic for Valium). "And, he upped my dose of the oxycodone (main ingredient in Percocet and oxycontin). He wants me taking four pills, five times a day now."

"Shit, Dad. That's too much. Holy shit. Let me see your arms," I said as I pulled his thin, long-sleeved shirt up. "Are you kidding me? You can't take all that shit, Dad. Look at your arms. You're gonna burn your house down, too. That's too much."

"It's not that bad, Tino. It's what the doctor wants and what he prescribed me."

His arms were covered in cigarette burns. As he nodded off, while sitting at the table, the cigarette clenched tightly between his brown bottom teeth and his top gum scalded his arms as his head fell toward sleep again and again. He'd jerk his head upright hundreds of times a day, but not before his skin scorched. Sometimes, though, not as often, the cigarette would fall from his teeth and gums and rest in the crook of his folded arms and burn, unnoticed, the length of the paper, to the butt. The process left a scab on both arms about two inches long.

For a week, while Greg McCarthy (my father's friend from Vietnam) was visiting him from New York, he fell out of his chair, spilled water, and passed out at the table. He slept for nearly the entire week of Greg's visit. On Greg's last day of his visit, we convinced my father to scrap the Soma and Valium. He wouldn't even consider a reduction in his opiates. I didn't push the subject.

I moved back in with him the following week.

\* \* \*

Part of the reason I moved back in with my father was to be with him, but my entire social network had also fallen apart. After Edwin and I returned from Hawaii I lost Brausa, and almost everyone in it. I was lonely.

A couple of days after we returned, Edwin called the mainstays at the gym—the leading group: Joe Riggs, John Lansing, me, and Jed, who came along for moral support. Edwin said Roland needed to start to pay us for our fights in Rage in the Cage, and get us a legit striking coach. We had all come to the same conclusion that Roland was using Brausa as a means to get a steady flow of fighters into the cage for him—which also meant the fighters friends and family would show up and pay money to watch, i.e. Roland was making bank off of us getting the shit kicked out of ourselves for free. Plus, I was teaching almost every class for Roland at that point, too. Over beers, in Edwin's tiny, dirty bungalow, we ranted on about all the changes we wanted to see at the gym. The group decided the next day we would all meet at Brausa at noon to speak with Roland.

In the morning, by the time Jed sauntered out of his bedroom, I had already left two messages on Edwin's phone, and one on John's.

"Edwin's not answering his phone. John, either," I said.

"Huh?"

"You know, to go speak with Roland today."

"Oh, yeah. That."

I got the impression that Jed assumed what was said the night before was just drunk talk and that no one intended to follow through with the changes, or more importantly, talk with Roland about them.

"I haven't talked with Joe, but he'll probably be there."

"Well, I'm not going if Edwin and John aren't going to be there."

"Bullshit!"

"What do I need to be there for? Roland doesn't give a shit what the hell I say." Jed was getting nervous.

"Goddammit, you're coming with me. Get fucking dressed."

"This is shit, Franco."

It was shit. All of it was. There I sat, going over the execution of a speech that was pushed to the forefront of my brain by people that weren't even there. I was fighting my own war, but I was also fighting for someone else. It just so happened that that "someone else" deserted the efforts and decided to stay home.

Jed did come with me. He also kept repeating that he didn't know why I wanted him there, as it didn't make a difference what he said. I knew that. He knew that. But we also knew he was supposed to be there for my support. He knew I was going to go through with the plan to get fair wages out of our factory boss—not just for me, but the whole union, and he didn't want anything to do with facing the owner of Brausa.

When we pulled in the parking lot, Joe was waiting in his small, green Nissan pickup truck. His shaved head appeared first, followed by his large, muscular frame.

"Ah, hell, Frank. I haven't been able to get a hold of Edwin all morning. Why don't we do this another time?" he said.

"Fuck that. If they want to bitch out, let them. Pussies," I replied.

We walked in and Roland was waiting for us. Jed told me that after I left Edwin's the previous night, Edwin called and left a message on Roland's voice mail, telling him we wanted to chat with him.

"I told you guys. I told you that you'd all come here someday asking me for money, trying to destroy my gym. They all leave. It's just a matter of time," Roland said.

"Roland, it's not like that at all," I said. "None of us want to leave. We just want to be paid to fight—just like every other show. And we want to be trained, or at least paid to teach."

"You think the grass is greener out there, Franco? You got a taste of money and now you think my pockets are full? Like I'm just rich over here and can afford to pay everyone?"

Jed and Joe sat on a bench with their heads down.

"It's not that. I mean, we get it. Rage in the Cage is your baby. That's where you make your money from, and we get that. But, we want to make it as fighters. I'm fine with you making money, but I want someone to train me—we want someone to train us—so we get where we want to be. If you making money with the fights happens to get me where I need to be as a fighter, great. I'd love to stay here. If it doesn't, then I'll have to go look out for myself, and find another place to train."

"What about you, Jed? Joe?" Roland asked.

"Ah—I—I don't know. I mean, whatever. I'm fine with things staying the way they are," Jed replied.

"Nah, Roland, we don't want to go," Joe said with his head down. "We ya know—we just want to get something."

"Franco, you think about this and let me know what you want to do. I can't promise you money, but I can make you a star. I can promote you like none of those other shows can. I can make you huge around here so the UFC sees you and gets you in."

I didn't mention that it was Edwin's idea and that all of us had conspired the evening prior. It wouldn't have made a difference.

I never trained at Brausa again. Nobody besides Joe even acknowledged that any of us wanted changes. Jonelle and I finally called it off. I left Jed's house to move back in with my father who, despite his insanity and our differences, always had his arms open for me. Beth was long gone. Chea was in New York. Adrianna was in Georgia. I was alone.

Back at my father's, I moped in my room.

"You okay, Teen?" my father said through the door.

"Yeah."

"Well, if you need anything, you can come out here with me at the table. I can see if anything's on TV."

"I'm fine."

"Well, okay. Goodnight, Teen."

I should have said yes.

# 14

Around the same time Seth and crew came over to train, Drew Fickett, another UFC fighter, also decided to call Southwest MMA (I figured that since we weren't technically on the west coast, we should change the name to correspond with the correct geographical location) home. With Drew came Efrain Escudero, a young wrestler.

Drew was a nightmare and I regularly told everyone, "Train with him, but don't get too close with him." He'll put beers for everyone in the bar on your tab then walk out on you and wonder why you're mad at him the next time you see him. He was a great fighter, but a madman of a human. To put it in perspective, the first time Drew was in a car with me, years prior to our time at Southwest MMA he startled me as we pulled up to a stop light and he calmly rolled his window down, stuck his head out the window, and proceeded to yell at a young woman.

"Whore! You fucking cock-sucking whore! Pussy juice, pussy juice, pussy juice!"

"What the hell are you doing? Do you know her?"

"No, but I bet she's a dirty, cock-sucking whore."

*Well, then, you may have a point. Continue on with your yelling, I suppose.*

Drew and I trained together at Arizona Combat Sports for some time, and during a road trip to New Mexico where a few of us were fighting at the time, Drew saw me reading *Atlas Shrugged* and started up a conversation.

"That's my mother's favorite book," Drew said.

I'd find out years later that his mother had died, and I think seeing that book in my hands, he somehow related me to his mother in some sense. He'd always listen to me in his fits of insanity, even when it made zero sense to do so. Now he was at my gym training after he'd been kicked out of all the other gyms in the city. Me and my retinue of miscreants were his last option.

The team was doing well. My fighters were taking fights all over the state and winning on a regular basis. It gave me a sense of accomplishment as a coach, but it pained me as a fighter. My competitive juices were still flowing. Training with the guys that were winning on the local level, and my ability to beat them at every facet of the fight game, made me think I was missing out on something. I started thinking I could still hang with the guys at the top. So what if every time I sparred I went home and had an anxiety attack; wondering if my head was going to explode.

I wanted to fight.

I thought I could fight.

In March of 2007, Kindal and I got married at her parents' house in Bullhead City, Arizona. We had planned to find a justice of the peace to marry us once we arrived in Hawaii, on our honeymoon. See, Kindal's entire family is Mormon (LDS), from her parents and siblings to her extended cousins and uncles. She was even raised LDS, but drifted from the church after she began attending college. I'm no man of religion, and I maintain, with certainty, that death brings us closer to nothing but the ground and the worms that find their way into us. The combination of my not caring about religion and Kindal's family being very religious didn't make us want to go through the logistics of a ceremony and waste money just so we could be uncomfortable with the situation. Plus, my friends and family would have enjoyed some booze to set the party off right—not so much her family's cup of tea.

About two weeks before the wedding her mother called and refused to allow us to get married in Hawaii and demanded we have a small ceremony at their house. There was no discussion about it: We were going to Bullhead City to get married, case closed. There were only a few invited guests. My friends Steve, (who sported a black eye and busted nose given to him by me during my bachelor party) and James drove from Phoenix with one of Kindal's friends—Kayla—who allowed them to drink whiskey the entire drive, and my sister Adrianna drove up with her husband, Ron. Besides those guests, the house was filled with her parents' church friends.

My only request was that the bishop marrying us, didn't say, "Until death do you part." I'd thought of it as such a morbid part of marriage. I wanted to believe our marriage could transcend time and space and bodies and life and death and continue for eternity: somewhere, somehow.

Of course the bishop included the "death do you part" line in our ceremony, along with a snide quip about someday being able to marry in the Temple to "seal our marriage for eternity"—something Mormons believe requires a person to be active in the church and to be eligible for temple visits.

My face flushed crimson with anger, but I held my tongue. After all, I was married to a woman that I loved, and I'd never see this pompous prick again.

Shortly after we got back from Hawaii, for whatever reason, I called my neurologist, Dr. McDougal.

"I wanted to know if Dr. McDougal would clear me to return to professional MMA competition?" I asked his secretary, Renee.

"I'll talk with Dr. McDougal and have him get back with you. Is there a fax number he could send his response to?"

I didn't have a fax at the gym, so I gave them Kindal's work fax number. The next day she called me from work. She was crying when I answered.

"What's wrong?" I asked.

"I just got a fax from Doctor McDougal. He cleared you to fight again—"

"He did? That's awesome!"

"What do you mean, that's awesome? What happens if you get hurt?"

"I won't. If he clears me, I'm fine. Don't do this. Don't be like that. This is all I ever wanted—to fight. And now I can do it again. Don't be selfish. I know you're scared, but everything's going to be fine."

I could see her point, though. We were married merely weeks prior, and here I was, planning to go get my head caved in, leaving her a widow. But I had to fight a demon. That demon wants to fulfill a dream. He's just too hungry. Too hungry to listen to logic or reason or his wife's crying voice on the other end of a phone. He wants his dream fulfilled. He doesn't care how he gets that, either.

And like that, I was back.

I didn't realize it at the time, but Kindal wasn't being selfish. Neither was I—though both might seem that way. As humans, we forget that we're all the center of our own universe. We say things like, "Why are you doing this to me?" but the reality is that nobody's doing anything to "you." We're doing things for ourselves. And the "you" just happens to overlap a bit with each person's "me."

Even bad people aren't doing things to deliberately harm others. It's all intrinsic selfishness that leads to harm. A Ponzi scheme operator isn't thinking, "I'm going to take all of these people's money and make them broke." He's thinking, "I can make a lot of money off of these people, and if it happens to hurt them, so be it." The same could be said for someone yelling at us—it's the person's anger or hurt or fear that leads to yelling—or even murder. Nobody just goes out and kills people, just to do it—not even serial killers. It has nothing to do with the victim, and all to do with the killer. It brings the killer happiness or solace or whatever it does to serial killers.

No, we as humans don't do things—good or bad— to others for any other reason than selfish ones. It's like we all have a circle around ourselves and our lives create an infinite number of Venn Diagrams. Every part of my own circle is a part of me, and each overlapping circle of someone else creates our own little "Universal Set" with someone else. Our circles can overlap a lot, even almost completely, but I will always have my own circle and everyone else will have their own dedicated circle.

It's not that anyone is ever really more selfish than anyone else. Some of us forget, or never figure out, that we're all separate from one another. Some people are just more aware of trying to appease the other Universal Sets, by making compromises, which keeps their own happiness level at a maximum.

So, when I help someone, it's because I care about my own relationship with that person enough that I want to keep it intact. If I do hurtful things, it means that my selfishness—what I want—is more important to me than my relationship with that person.

It's all point of view. There are no good guys or bad guys. Everyone's a good guy in his or her own mind. There are just different sides of the war.

No, neither of us were being selfish, we just had different centric circles that we wanted to keep happy. Hers consisted of a healthy husband that she loved, but a happy one. Mine consisted of a happy self, that could earn a living at fighting, which would help me provide for my wife and family, when the time came.

Prior to my two-year hiatus from competition, I'd amassed a record of 10-2 as a professional, including a win over Melvin Guillard, who was now a successful fighter in the UFC. So, when I announced to the MMA world that I was back, the offers came flooding in: from the UFC to fight Din Thomas, an ever-tough veteran of the sport; an offer from the up-and-coming promotion the International Fight League, an organization that pitted city teams against one another similar to other professional sports; and an offer from Bodog Fights, an MMA show run by Bodog gambling site founder, Calvin Ayre. I wasn't certain of the route I wanted to take. The UFC was the UFC, but did I want my first fight back from brain surgery to be in the largest, most prominent promotion in the world? The IFL was going to pay me a lot of money, including a monthly salary in addition to my pay and win bonuses, but I'd have to fight every six weeks, and I didn't have much say in my opponents, as it was team versus team. Then there was Bodog, the most unrecognizable show, but with the best pay.

One of the caveats with the IFL that I'd brought on board, though, was that I'd consider fighting for them, if Don Frye, the coach of the IFL's

Tucson Scorpions would take Seth as their 185-lb fighter, a spot vacant due to an injury.

Don agreed to consider Seth if he would be willing to do some sparring with Don, and Scorpions team member, Mike Whitehead. We eagerly agreed, and off to Tucson for training we went.

With most MMA organizations, the matchmaker looks at fight videos and the professional record of the fighter to decide if he wants to sign him or not. Maybe he makes some phone calls to ask about the fighter, or maybe videos and strength of his opponents is enough to sign new fighters—it all depends on the mood of the matchmaker that day. The IFL was different, though. The International Fight League was the first—and to my knowledge the only—MMA organization that was based on a team concept. Each team was based out of city, much like NFL or NBA teams, and the coaching staff got to choose the fighters for each weight class that would represent them, respectively. So, if we could convince Don that Seth was worth his weight in salt, we had a solid chance to get Seth the big breakthrough we were all looking for.

After two hours in a car Seth, my friend Cade, a giant Mexican named Joe (he's 6'5" 250-lbs), and I arrived at the Tucson Scorpions training center and were greeted by Steve and Don. Mike Whitehead was probably in the back somewhere with a scowl on his face warming up, as that is generally the face Whitehead chooses to wear. Nothing seemed too out of the ordinary, except for the fact that Don was wearing purple spandex that went from his waist to his ankles and a pair of wrestling shoes. Nothing else set off any alarms at the time, though he did have enough chest hair to be mistaken for a sweater.

Cade and I went over to warm up and do some technique with a lighter fighter, Ed West, who I would have been replacing had I decided to join the Scorpions. Seth was wrapping his hands and asked if they were going to be wearing headgear?

"Of course we are wearing head gear. We're going to be hitting each other in the face," Don replied with his gravelly voice.

After the squad was suited up, Seth foolishly began to shadow box and warm up.

"Save your energy for the ring, boy," Don snarled, and Seth obliged the man that was now wearing wrestling shoes, purple tights, and headgear. Don's head looked like a Smurf with a moustache. His headgear was so tight that it made his already red face turn a shade of purple or maybe blue. To make it better, whenever Don would grumble something, his moustache would move up and down like whiskers on a laughing hyena. You couldn't really see his mouth though, so it looked like a purple face with a 'stache and two beady little eyes poking out from inside the headgear.

Cade, Ed, and I were keeping an inconspicuous watch on the ring to see the goings on, but we were supposed to be working out too, so we didn't pull chairs up to the ring and whip out bags of popcorn.

The sparring began and Seth was in first with Don. Seth looked like a deer in headlights. His tall gangly arms resembled Popeye's wife, Olive Oil, more than a fighter. To say Seth was a little nervous would be an atrocious understatement. He was in the ring, sparring with *the* MMA legend, Don Frye. Nevertheless, Seth was doing pretty well. He flicked some jabs at Don, which snapped his purple-smurf-stache-face back a few times. But, after a few jabs, Don was no longer interested in "working" and began to throw bombs at Seth's head. The two exchanged hard shots and Don finished the round pinning Seth in the corner of the ring going punch for punch.

After the round ended Don asked, "What size gloves are those, 10's?"

Seth replied, "16 oz."

"Don't lie to me, boy. Those are tiny. Steve, get me some smaller gloves," Don called out. "Kid's trying to take my head off or something." All the time he was winking at everyone around as if he's letting us in on something.

Round two began for Seth and he was now in the ring with Mike Whitehead, who probably out-weighed Seth by forty pounds. Mike was swinging at Seth like Seth said something bad about his mother, and he even threw in a double leg takedown for good measure, even though it was, to Seth's knowledge, just boxing sparring.

Don screamed at everyone and anyone in the gym, "STOP, STOP!"

"We need a ref! We need a Goddamn referee in here!"

I certainly didn't want any part of what was going on in the ring, so I tried to avoid eye contact with the giant angry man running the show.

"You!" he said, pointing at me. "Come here you little pencil neck faggot, get your ass in here and referee this shit!"

Well, that was my cue, and in to the ring I went. The round was reset and punching resumed. After a minute or so, Seth and Whitehead clinched and I yelled, "Break!" putting my hands on each of their shoulders. I broke them up from clinching as much as I could, but it began to get a little dirty in the clinch. Mike was still punching Seth even after I tried to break them up. He snapped short head-butts at Seth to make sure he knew who the king was.

The round ended and Frye screamed at me, "Come here! When you break us up you get your ass in between us, and fucking break us up! We're trying to hurt each other in there. It's a goddamn dogfight in there. You got me?"

I did get him.

After a couple more rounds of them putting Seth through the gauntlet, he got to sit a round out and Don and Mike were showing each other how much they cared for one another by exchanging right hands to the face, neither caring much for defense.

Before he could catch his breath, Seth was back in against Mike, and Mike seemed to be tiring a bit. The round began, and Seth started to land clean shots to his opponent. Annoyed, Mike went back to his wrestling days and tripped Seth in almost every clinch. The dirty clinch work of Whitehead came to a boiling point when he decided he didn't want Seth to hit him in the face any further, and hip tossed Seth over the top rope and out of the ring.

I don't know how Don did it, as it was a thing miracles are made of, but he somehow jumped over the top rope of the ring so fast it was as if he teleported to the middle of the ring. This is even more amazing as both of Don's knees are shot and he doesn't do anything remotely fast.

"What the hell are you doing?" screamed Don, to Mike. "You don't do that shit! You get out of my gym, you get out of Tucson, and you get the hell out of Arizona! You're off my fucking team!"

The training session was officially over. After a few minutes Whitehead began packing his things. Seth was completely exhausted wondering what the hell was going on. Cade and I exchanged wow-that-was-completely-crazy glances back and forth and Big Joe was hiding out somewhere so as to not be involved in any of the calamity. All of us were completely dumbfounded by the circus we had just been a part of.

A few minutes later Cade, Seth, Big Joe, and I were sitting around in an awkward silence when Don came out of the back room.

"I'm sorry," he said in a loud voice. "This was all my fault and I'm sorry. I let this get out of hand. Mike, get your ass back over here. You're not off the team. You can stay. I shouldn't have let this get out of hand like this."

After we had collected our things and were heading out the door to head back to Phoenix, Don mumbled to Seth, "Ya got heart, kid." And gave him a wink for the road.

## 15

    Peter James DeFranco was born in Watertown, New York, to Rocco and Betty DeFranco, though he told our mother he was born in Sicily. He was raised in an Italian household until he became of legal age, and moved to California to attend the Catholic Seminary. He questioned the priests for answers, but only received, "God will answer your questions when it is time," for a response and grew frustrated with his education.
    Well, that's the story he had always told my sisters and me, but I think it may have had more to do with his meeting a woman, Annette, who was attending the adjacent nunnery at the time. When he left the seminary, Annette conveniently decided the life of a nun was not for her, and they married. He then entered the U.S. Army and was eventually shipped off to Vietnam, while Annette reared their four children: Marty, Kevin, Cathy, and Charlene. Eventually, he and Annette got divorced due to his excessive drinking, and his absence while deployed. He barely saw Annette or any of the children of his first marriage (outside of Cathy) again.
    After his days of Purple Hearts, Bronze Stars, and Presidential Citations were behind him for his acts of valor on the battlefield, he enrolled in university and started working on his PhD in Psychology, which is where he met my mother, Saundra. They wed and shortly after, Chea (named after Che Guevara, whom my father had a hand in helping the Bolivian government catch, then tried to convince them not to kill him, as told by a Green Beret that knew my father—Pete wouldn't talk about his military service), Adrianna, and I were born.
    He may have left his old family behind, but he certainly didn't leave the torment and anguish of Vietnam with them. I'm sure that war psychologically scarred everyone that had a thing to do with it, but my father's was an overly exceptional case of torment. Beside the fact that he

was a decorated Green Beret that was in Cambodia and Laos before we were really "in Cambodia and Laos" and that he had been a prisoner of war, or that he saw the real gritty shit that the Green Berets and other elite groups saw, the real torment that haunted him rose from his religious background and his need to find some sort of balance between the two. He went from wanting to become a priest and serving God for the rest of his life to killing for a living in a very short amount of time. As an adult, I started poking around at the idea of having his service medals reissued (he had thrown them all away when we were very young) so I could put them in a nice shadow box and give them to him for a present. His response was, "What do I deserve medals for? For killing women and children? I don't deserve any medals for that." He once told me he wondered if he'd spend eternity in hell. I didn't know.

His religious beliefs, though they pulled his soul in all directions, helped us escape the trailer that we had been living in for almost two years. Somehow a group of Jehovah's Witnesses stumbled upon our trailer one day and my father invited them in. Almost immediately we were attending their services regularly and having weekly meetings with them in our home. From then on, we didn't celebrate birthdays or Christmas for a few years, and we had to stop saying the Pledge of Allegiance in elementary school, which I thought was fun as I got to stay sitting during the weird ritual.

Life quickly moved much further from what we were used to quickly after the Jehovah's Witnesses entered our lives. They convinced my father to move us to government low-income housing, which he did. Then they convinced him to go to a Veterans Administration rehab program, which he did. When he came out, he was clean and sober for the first time in our lives and the VA in Canandaigua, New York, hired him as a therapist to treat other Veterans. We then went on a series of moves that would continue until I was done with high school.

We moved to a motel in Canandaigua, then to a small apartment above a sports bar. Then there was the cottage rental on the lake. It was cold all year around, but our neighbor worked for a candy company and would give us giant garbage bags full of candy. We lived there for a year before we moved to Geneva, New York. Three houses in Geneva found us under their roofs before we moved to Freeville, and it continued on and on.

Even though he ran from the world, and we ran with him, our father always took Chea, Adrianna, and me with him. We'd pack up as quickly as we unpacked, and be gone in a flash. Some of the places we lived were a step up, some a step down. There was no rhyme or reason to his movements. Maybe he was running to protect us? Or himself? Maybe he was running from the people he knew or chasing those he didn't know.

Maybe he was running from himself, and thought he could somehow outrun his shadow?

During the periods of constant movement, he stopped working. He became involved with some litigious mess with the Veterans Administration (that he won years later) and then he was once again at the comfort of his kitchen table every moment he wasn't sleeping on the couch. As abruptly as his short stint as a working adult came, it went. I never saw my father work again. Some days he was slurring his words between bouts of yelling in Vietnamese or Spanish, or shooting holes in the ceiling, while sloppy on the anti-psychotics the doctors prescribed him. Other days he would yell at us and ground us for months on end for something as trivial as not taking out the garbage. The groundings had much less to do with our misbehavior than it did with him trying to keep us close to him, but, eventually, we didn't care.

## 16

Seth was taken on as the 185-lb fighter for the Scorpions, but I decided to sign with Bodog, who was paying me too much money to turn down.

I called Don Frye to tell him that I'd be turning down the spot on his team to fight in Bodog. I figured he'd understand as Bodog was paying great money and I could have more say in my opponents.

"You gave me your word, boy," he grumbled into the phone after I told him.

"But you of all people should understand that it's better for my career to fight in Bodog. It's good money and I can pick my opponents."

"Well, I don't understand. A man's word is his word. You gave me your word and then went and did something else. There's no honor in that. If you got no honor, I don't want you on my team anyway."

Very well, then.

So, I wouldn't be fighting with Seth in the IFL, but I was still certain Bodog was the right choice—the only issue, though, was that I would be fighting in three weeks and flying to St. Petersburg, Russia, in two. Not only did I have to cancel my wedding reception, which my estranged mother had already bought her airline ticket to travel to Phoenix for, but I had to corner Drew Fickett in Vegas against Keita Nakamura, and get myself and Seth ready for fights occurring only a day apart. My cardio was shit, I had barely sparred in years, and I was afraid to get hit, on top of all of that, I didn't have a trainer, but was training myself with my other fighters. It was the worst possible scenario any fighter in my situation could imagine, and I couldn't have been happier.

I flew to Vegas the day before Drew's fight to corner him along with Andy Wang against Nakamura. Our room situation was less than ideal, as both beds had multiple people in them, and I was relegated to the floor. A pillow and blanket were my sleeping grounds, but I was fine with that.

When we got to the arena on fight day, Drew pulled two cans of beer from his bag and an empty sports-squirt-bottle.

"What's your plan with that?" I asked.

"I'm gonna drink these beers before my fight. I feel like I always do better in sparring if I have a few beers in me."

"That's a really bad idea, Drew."

Andy agreed with me, but Drew wasn't one to be swayed.

It was a bad idea, but I envied Drew for his crazy. He didn't care about getting hurt. He didn't care about each and every detail of the fight. He certainly didn't scrutinize every daily decision and wonder if it would affect his health or brain. He had a freedom that I'd never known. It was crazy freedom, but it was freedom. I don't suggest anyone go and try to live their life by the fuck-it-I'm-doing-shit-my-way-regardless-of-the-ramifications way that Drew does, but to not give a fuck. And I'm not talking about the people that act crazy or a certain way so people say, "he doesn't give a fuck." I'm not talking about the hipsters that say they don't like corporate because they can't be corporate or because they want people to "know how cool and careless he is." To truly not give a fuck is amazing. Scary, but amazing.

"Seriously, bro, I swear, the more I drink, the more relaxed I am while sparring. Trust me, I'll be fine," Drew said.

And, so, that was that. Drew started drinking about an hour or so before we were set to begin his warm up. Fortunately, after about half of the beer was gone, he stopped.

"Yeah, I think you guys were right. That was a really bad idea. You think one of you could run and grab me some coffee?"

I was more than happy to see him fall victim to the "correct" category of vice and I got up and ran to the Starbucks in the hotel. When I returned with a triple shot of espresso, he quickly poured it down his throat. To his credit, he did win the fight, and looked pretty impressive doing so, too. That was his last fight in the UFC, though. His out of cage antics eventually got him 86'd for life.

After the fight he wanted me to go party with him and his friends. I graciously declined and went back to our hotel room with Andy and hung out for a while before getting to my floor space to sleep. I had a journey to Great Mother Russia. I couldn't be out gallivanting about in Vegas.

\*\*\*

## April 2007:

I was flying alone. Cade Swallows, my corner man, was going to meet me in Russia the day before the fight, since he had to work as a Phoenix firefighter for most part of the week. He was by no means qualified to corner or coach, but at the time I didn't really have a coach, so I figured I'd bring a friend to Russia for the experience. He wasn't a complete MMA virgin, though. He had a couple of fights of his own under his belt, and even fought some tough opponents, but I could have definitely chosen a more qualified candidate for the position.

When the day came for my departure, Kindal dropped me off at the airport and I met up with Steve Steinbeiss and his brother Ray, who were also fighting on the same card. We stopped at a Subway to grab a sandwich before our flight and then headed to our terminal.

Sitting in my aisle seat, I was still surprised that I was able to get a visa to Russia in just a few days. I'd read online that it could take months to be approved for entry into the country. I would later find out that the Russian Mafia runs everything from politics to visas. When the flight attendant started yapping on the loudspeaker I took a sleeping pill, and when I woke up, I was in Helsinki, Finland, and then off to St. Petersburg, Russia.

\* \* \*

After a short time at customs in St. Petersburg, we found our driver and climbed into his van. He was a tall bald man and he met us with three other men—most in leather jackets with stout frames and a slickness to them that said *gangster*. Driving into the city we saw buildings—old buildings—the size of city blocks one after the other. The buildings weren't tall. Most were two to four stories, but the massive amount of ground they took up was amazing. Our driver told us that the Russians wanted to show their architectural abilities when Napoleon was building France up. The Russian czars built endlessly to compete with the small French man. Apparently, the country's money was being spent on the buildings while the people starved, but I have not substantiated this. I hope it's true because it made the buildings seem even larger than they were; being part of a time of strife and peril for the workers, but a time of development for the country. Our van finally arrived in front of our hotel and we disembarked wondering what type of place we would be staying in as guests in this foreign land.

It was spectacular.

The entrance was filled with people checking in for the fights and acquiring meal tickets for the restaurant buffet, which we were allowed to eat at for free. The large chandelier was platinum and sparkled with crystal that shone silver like the moon. There was a coffee shop and bar at the top of a small set of stairs where beautiful Russian women were mingling with martinis in their hands. I was in Great Mother Russia and I was happy to be there, but I also scared. My presence in Russia meant I would fight again. I was going to test the coils and stent that kept the aneurysm from rupturing between my ears; to see whether the craftsmanship of my neurosurgeon was worthy of my recommendation to another fighter if he found himself in need of brain repair. Or if my doctor's workmanship would render me dead, or in need of medical attention so far from home, where Barrows Neurological Center is only a quick ambulance ride away.

We were shown to our rooms and our bags were handled for us. I opened the door to a room suited for a richer man. After my things were unpacked, I went back downstairs where I met my Phoenix crew for a walk around the city. We had five days before we had to weigh in, six days until we fought, and on the seventh day, we would return home, so we certainly weren't planning on holing up in the hotel for the entirety of our stay.

Steve was the tallest of the bunch and I spotted him first. He was standing next to the other two and waved to me. Ray, Steve's brother, older but shorter, who was also fighting on the card had a court jester's grin on his face and was staring wide-eyed at everything in his view. Todd Lally, their trainer, a bald ginger, had a red goatee and reminded me of an MMA trainer version of Rumpelstiltskin. The four of us exited into the cold.

We walked toward the town center, with its bazaars and restaurants, and people on the streets everywhere. The people were a cold lot. They wore greys and blacks and blues and I'm certain that clothes made with yellow, green, or red may have been grounds for death if worn on the frigid, grey streets. The people didn't look up when they walked. If they did, they certainly didn't smile. They were the lost souls one reads about in Dostoyevsky or Tolstoy. These were their people, and each and every one of them was true to form. They looked tired, freezing, and miserable. They reminded me of my youth in upstate New York in a trailer near the Canadian border without running water, electricity, heat, or any other amenity the $20^{th}$ century had to offer.

The difference, though, was I was young and excited and knew the world had much to offer. I had seen Nintendos, and fast, expensive cars. I knew that people could make a name for themselves in America, and there was a social and economic ladder to climb. I did not personally have any of those things, nor did I see the ascent of status and income from my father, but I knew it was there. I had seen it on TV, I had read about it in school, and heard it on the radio. The Russians, they did not have any shooting stars in their sky to wish on. Their ladder had one rung on it, which was just high enough to reach for one more day of living at a time.

After an hour the cold got to us, as we bought our coats in the desert of Phoenix. One should always buy supplies for severe weather where severe weather takes place, or in this day and age, on the internet. We apparently were ill informed and, thus, were inadequately prepared. Red-nosed, cheeked, and finger tipped, we arrived back at our hotel, the antithesis of the sad, somber streets we had recently explored. The hotel was a farce, an insult to those living around it. The hotel, and the wealth of the buildings, was a water fountain in the desert that only the kings could use, but I was certainly not unhappy spending my nights there.

Back at the hotel, we decided a meal would be the best thing to pass the time and take the cold from our bones and we approached the restaurant with its great spread. They had pasta with Milanese sauce, prime rib, and a slew of pork dishes. There were mashed potatoes with ham and bacon in them, and a ton of other sides. I hadn't eaten beef or pork or any other form of red meat since I was 15 years old, but fortunately, I brought three boxes of oatmeal with me in case something as startling as only having meat on the menu occurred. My good planning worked in my favor. And though I couldn't eat much of the food, I did enjoy coffee by the carafe. Since I still had five days until weigh-ins, and was only ten pounds over weight, I had a small piece of chocolate mousse cake. Over coffee and oatmeal and cake, Steve told me of his previous journey to Russia to fight for the same organization. The promoters would call museums in the middle of the night and have them opened for the fighters. They would make a call, and Russian army special forces would show up with automatic weapons and tanks if they wanted props for shooting video. As we were about to leave the table, a Japanese reporter came up to us and started chatting.

"Who are each of you fighting?" he asked, and we gave him our names and those of our opponents.

"Nice, nice. You will all do very well. Have you been out to see the city at all?" he asked in very well-spoken English.

"Yeah, earlier," Todd said. "We're thinking about heading back out in a bit once we're warmed up. You know, check out the place at night. See if there's any cool places around."

"I would be very careful about going out around here at night."

"Is this a bad neighborhood?" I asked. "It looks decent."

"No, it's not the people that live near here you need to be worried about, but the cops. The cops robbed some of the fighters that came in last night when they were out—just a few blocks from here. Don't make eye contact with them and try to avoid them if you can."

We decided we'd be better off going to our rooms and waiting for daylight again for any Columbus escapades.

Up in my room, I paced back and forth for hours. The time difference was jarring and I was wide awake. I was alone in Russia and the butterflies fluttered through my gut as my mind drifted into thoughts about dying after taking a punch to the brain, which is about ten times the amount of butterflies that generally accumulate in the belly during fight week. I was wide awake without the comfort of sleep to mask my anxieties anytime soon. Hell, I couldn't even pretend to watch TV as it was all in an angry sounding language!

During the days I hung out with Steve, Ray, and Todd, and wandered the streets, taking in the city of the great writers. At night, I did laps in my room and thought of my mortality and my new wife while going back and forth from shadow boxing and pushups and trying to sleep when the moon showed herself.

When Friday finally arrived, I was by no means worried about my weight. The abundance of dishes containing creatures that graze kept me from eating almost anything the entire week besides copious amounts of coffee. So, with my weight barely five pounds over and still hours before the weigh-ins, I decided to walk the streets one last time and grab a cup of coffee a few blocks from the hotel at a little café I'd frequented throughout the week. The wind was stronger than in the previous days, and the chill got to me quickly. I was nearly jogging when I saw a little boy clawing at his mother's shoulder trying to get her attention, but to no avail. He began sobbing and yelling something at her in Russian, but I couldn't decipher the words. The woman seemed asleep as if she was drugged or dead and it reminded of the days in the trailer.

I was no older than six years old when we found our dogs as the spring thaw began to set in. I don't know how we got the dogs, or even remember their names. They were some sort of lab mixture—black and white—and were brother and sister if I recall correctly. We hadn't seen them for the entire winter and we assumed they ran into the woods to find food and refuge from the harsh weather. One day we were behind our yellow trailer meddling about and I happened to look beneath our home and saw the two dogs coiled up together like snakes, frozen stiff. The male still had his teeth showing as if he was snarling at the death of winter until his last breath turned into ice on its way out of his lungs for the last time.

A few days later, still shaken up by the odd sight of the frozen dogs, my father decided my sisters and I would accompany him on a long walk in the woods. We had a beaver pond about a half a mile or so behind the trailer, in the middle of the forest, miles from town, and he wanted to see if it began to thaw or not in hopes that we could begin to take water from it to boil, and then drink.

We bundled ourselves up and began walking toward the pond. In the summer we could smell the giant raspberries growing on bushes from around the corner, yards away, and we would smile with anticipation of painting our hands and faces red by the treats. The berries had yet to come back from the winter, though, and when we reached the pond it was still frozen, but there was a small amount of water collected on top of the ice that was melted off by the spring heat. My sisters and I played tag and threw twigs at each other and ignored my father's grumbles. When we turned to go back to the trail we had taken to get to the pond, my father, not thrilled about the absence of a water supply, decided to take a different route through unfamiliar woods back to our trailer. We walked in what seemed to be circles, for what seemed to be hours, until my father eventually sat down on a rock that was shoved deep into the side of a hill and was free of the remaining winter snow. He began to breathe heavily and grab at his chest.

"I don't feel good, guys," he said, then laid his head on the hill next to him.

"Are you okay? What's wrong, Dad?" my sisters said with teary eyes.

"I think I'm dying. It's my heart. I don't know how to get back and we're lost. I think I'm dying."

We ran to him, swarming him like flies on horses' eyes in the heat of summer. We hugged him and scratched at his lifeless face and told him we loved him. We screamed and raged, hugging him more and shaking his lifeless body and begged him to be okay—to be alive. Then we screamed again that we loved him so much that he must be okay.

After a few minutes of our little fingers kneading and clawing at him his eyes opened and he became lucid. We were beyond thankful and relieved that our father had not died and left us three orphans in the harsh world, alone to fend for ourselves. Almost immediately, he knew exactly where we were, and within minutes we were home—back inside, with the kerosene stench of our trailer, warm and happy, though shaken up. That was by no means the last time he fraudulently told us he was dying. There was cancer, his heart, Agent Orange, and a great many others.

When the Russian mother's eyes opened and she hugged her child on the streets of St. Petersburg, all I could think of was what a pity it was that she was not dead. Over the course of a lifetime, she'd do more damage to him than good. But she was just trying to live—to live her life, her own circle, and her son was just a Universal Set overlapping hers.

I sipped my coffee at the café slowly and thought about my internal fight to enter the ring after such a long lay-off. I also thought of my actual fight and just wanted to *fight*. I didn't want to go for a takedown and force my opponent to submit—to tap out—like I had in most of my previous fights. I didn't care about winning or losing, or looking good or bad. I wanted to punch and kick and hit another man and have him hit me and see if I stood before him alive or lay at his feet dead when the limbs settled.

I didn't care about fighting Rodrigo Damm in Russia on Pay-Per-View while my wife was at home with my mother, who flew to Arizona to celebrate our wedding (while I flew across the world and didn't see her.) I didn't care that I was the favorite in the fight or that he was a national wrestling champion in Brazil. I didn't care that I had trained for the fight for just a week with sub-par training partners while taking nearly a two-year lay-off.

As I finished my coffee by myself in the land of Grushenka and Margharita and Raskolnikov, the only thing I cared about was fighting. Getting in the ring and fighting. As the Russian in Rocky IV said, "If he dies, he dies." But most of all, I didn't want to be scared. I didn't want to be scared to fight. Scared to get hit. I was so nervous since my brain had failed me. In life—just so nervous. *Is this headache the death of me? Did that punch rupture the aneurysm?* I didn't want those thoughts anymore.

I wanted to just fight.

Winning and losing and fighting was just the medium in which I would be able to display my strength or fears before the world, and, more importantly, myself.

\* \* \*

Cade's trip was not as leisurely as mine. He arrived the evening before the fight, after the weigh-ins, and was flying out with me two days later. His dark brown hair and Midwestern drawl offered me comfort in the land of strangeness I'd been living in for five days.

Over breakfast on fight day I was graced by all the gods in all the lands when I saw waffles at the buffet instead of a myriad of meat dishes. I doused butter and syrup over my meat-free carbs, to soften the crispness.

"You know all that butter's going to kill you, right?" Cade said.

"But sometimes dying tastes good," I said.

"What's your plan tonight? You're a lot better on the feet than him. You gonna keep it standing?"

"Yeah." I nodded my head in affirmation. "I saw him fight Kultar and I don't think he can beat me standing. I don't even know if he can take me down. I wasn't really impressed with his wrestling. It's in a ring, too—it'll be hard for him to get me down."

"Yeah, I figured as much. You ready?" Cade asked, his voice moving up an octave.

"As ready as I'll ever be."

\* \* \*

We were in the arena early. The cement floors didn't help the chill in the air of the hockey stadium turned MMA venue. There were armed men with machine guns, and when we inquired why we were told that Vladimir Putin was planning on attending the event with some other international politicians and Jean-Claude Van Damme.

"Van Damme? Really?" we all asked, curious about how the hell that had come about.

In the warm-up room we were told we could only use nine feet of tape and nine feet of gauze to wrap our hands—which is not a lot of either. I began warming up before the first fight started. Cade and I pummeled, and I shadow-boxed and hit mitts with Rumpelstiltskin, who was also kind enough to wrap my hands, and lend us a corner bucket. I was severely underprepared. Midway through the first fight I walked from the warmup room into the main arena and saw thousands of fans screaming in their seats. The arena held 16,000 people, and judging by the empty-seat to full-seat ratio, it was a near sellout. My heart raced and my stomach sunk and I took deep breaths and clenched my jaw and continued to shadow box as I went backstage. Just before I got out of the arena I heard a big BANG. The crowd roared. Someone had delivered a blow. The crowd thirsted for more.

The time passed slowly. I was ready to face my opponent and the only thing left in my way was the clock. The seconds, ticking one-by-one, eventually reached a minute, and then to five minutes, which signaled the end of the first round. There was a minute in between rounds and then the second round began. The clock ticked once again. I shadow boxed and paced like a caged tiger that knows the door is about to open. Five more minutes and the end of the second round had come. Another minute break. I waited. I breathed deeply.

"Come on, Tino! You're ready for this! You know what to do, brother. Now just go out there and do it," Cade said.

The third round started, but before the final bell the fight was over—TKO victory for someone. I didn't care who won. I just cared that I was up.

Before I could go out there, though, there was the pomp and circumstance of announcing the winner and having the previous fighters exit the ring and return backstage, which took forever. The locker rooms were far from the ring at the edge of the arena. The ring, which was in the middle of thousands of screaming Russians could only be accessed by the fighters by a long pathway that went in between the fans.

I quickly made my way to the door and waited for the usher to take me to the ring, but there was an issue. The ropes had to be tightened before the next fight—my fight. The first fighter, the loser from Finland, came back into my corner with blood streaming down his face. He immediately went to the shower toward the back of the locker room and began to vomit.

"We need to get him to a hospital," his corner said in broken English.

"We're in Russia, man. You're not going to a hospital here. There are no hospitals in Russia, man. Not that you want to go to, anyways," someone yelled back. His cornerman made the sign of the cross and held a Rosary necklace.

*Faith. I wish I had that.*

At some point I did have it—faith, that is. Well, I don't know if I had actual faith, but I had fear. The fear of the hellfire and brimstone that comes along believing in God, and more terrifying, the Devil and demons and the such.

My father never expressed his faith outwardly, but he did force us to practice religion. While we were living in the trailer, we attended a Catholic school for a time, maybe a year and a half. We didn't pay for it, of course, we were a charity case. As with almost everyone that attends Catholic school, I hated it. We had the ubiquitous Catholic uniform that had to be worn daily, which, though we didn't have many other clothing options, I always hated having to wear. But more-so than the uniforms, I hated, absolutely hated, having to go to church. Everything about the Bible to me was frightful. I didn't get much of the love and peace and goodness-leads-to-heaven out of it. No, I got the version that highlighted the nefarious, malevolent aspect of the good book. All I got from the scriptures was that demons were after my soul and would take it any chance they got and drag me to hell for eternity. That, coupled with having watched *Nightmare on Elm Street* when I was six, led me down a path of fear for years to come. Fortunately, our attendance at the school was short-lived, but my discomfort with the Catholic Bible maintained.

Shortly after our exit from the Catholic school, we became Jehovah's Witnesses. During a door-to-door outing, where the JW's knock on doors to preach the scriptures, a family saw our trailer from the woods. Surprisingly, our father was all open ears and welcomed them into our lives. We attended their church services numerous time a week and walked door-to-door alongside them. Although we worshipped with them, we were not one of them. Our father continued to smoke cigarettes, despite the church banning the habit. We also continued to celebrate birthdays and other holidays. We just didn't mention those to the JWs. Eventually, my sisters and I convinced our father that we were not Jehovah's Witnesses, and we no longer wanted to be a part of the church.

And that was the end of my organized religion. I don't know if I'd ever believed in God, or if I was just afraid that if there was a God then there was probably all of the scary things that can accompany a God: the need to worship a God, a Devil, religious rules that should be followed. I once had a dream when I was around sixteen or seventeen where I asked God if he existed. He answered me and said yes, but not in the way that we thought. He said we were all just energy, and that we were all connected through our energy. The energy in the inanimate and the living all contained the same type of materials—atoms, consisting of electrons, protons, and neutrons—and that we were all connected through said energy. When I woke up, I sort of believed that. I sort of believed there was some sort of God, maybe not one that engages in intelligent design, but something.

Now, as I look back, I don't know if I still believe any of that. I want to believe that. I want to believe in something. I think it's easier. I envy those that believe that there's something more to this life than what is here, because it means we're eternal. But I don't think we're that special. I don't think we're eternal. I think we're just lucky to be here for the short time that we're here and when we're gone, we're gone. Part of the reason I'd always sought to achieve some sort of greatness that would live on after my death. It was my way of staying alive just a little longer. Maybe we're the gods. Maybe our energy travels through the universe unseen like something out of the Matrix. The lines of atoms and sub-atomic particles prance around unseen, unknown, all around us mocking us with their existence. Maybe they and us and all of it make up some sort of living being that extends beyond us. Just maybe, but I doubt it. So there's always another way: achieve something beyond ourselves for others to talk about after we die.

"Santino, you're up!"

Faith couldn't save me, and it didn't seem to be saving the fighter that was vomiting blood all over the open shower room. No, faith could do nothing. I'd have to fight my way out of this one. I went to the edge of the crowd and waited for my name to be called by the ring announcer.

*Come on, come on. Hurry up!* I thought.

"And, in the red corner, SANTINO DEFRANCO!"

My entrance music started and I began to make my way to the ring. As I walked, I bounced slowly to the cage, raising my hands and shadow boxing for the crowd. I slapped the many hands that were clawing out at me. Walking out to the cage happens in slow motion and in the eternal moments in my head I saw the mullets of the Russian men and the round faces of the women. I saw a tall man that stretched further than human genetics should allow and a red stone ring on a finger of a woman near me. I finally made my way to my corner and Cade pulled my shirt over my head and took my shoes. A cut man applied Vaseline on my face and the ref asked if I had my mouthpiece and backhanded my groin to make sure an athletic cup was underneath my shorts. Turning toward the ring, I saw Vladimir Putin and Jean-Claude Van Damme in the front row *I guess they really are here!* I jumped in the ring and held my hands high and paraded around, giving the crowd the show they were there for. As the announcer introduced us again I felt naked. The sweat that accumulated during my warm up was now exposed to the cold air. Thousands of eyes were staring at me in the arena and millions more at home, around the world, on Pay-Per-View. My opponent, Rodrigo Damm, a Brazilian that looked like steroids were snacks stared at me from the other side of the ring.

"In the blue corner, weighing one hundred and fifty-six pounds, with a record of..." *I don't give a damn! Hurry up, dammit!*

The announcer yelled to the crowd my weight of 156lbs and accolades, including my record of 11-2, but all I heard was *blah, blah, blah* as I stared at my foe as he jumped around in his corner waiting for the gates to release us into the derby. The announcer finished. He left the ring. Rodrigo and I were brought to the center of the ring for our last instructions and to touch gloves.

The bell rang. "FIGHT!" yelled the referee.

My nerves were gone.

Low kick. Slip the overhand and come back with a right. BANG! *He has a good right.* CRACK! *His low kick is good.*

Move in and out. Middle kick. Middle kick again.

Circle out of the corner. Jab. Jab. Low kick. CRACK!

*He's better on the feet than I thought.* Move. 1-2-3 combo and a low kick. SMACK!

Ding. Ding. Round one is over.

"Tino, it was a close round, but he may have won it. How do you feel?"

"Good. You think he won that round? Hmm, I thought I won it."

"Work for the take down."

"Got it. Let me have some more water."

Ding. Ding. Round two.

Feint. Jab. Move. CRACK! *I saw lights on that one.* Shoot for the takedown.

SHIT! He's on my back with his arm around my neck. Loss of blood to brain.

Tap out. Lose fight. Breathe.

Overcome fear.

Rejoice!

Leave the ring.

Live.

I wasn't even angry that I had lost. Because I didn't. I won. I went in the ring and fought. I didn't face Rodrigo Damm that night in Russia, I stared myself in the eyes through a round and a half of battle. I wasn't scared of getting hit. I wasn't scared of dying. I didn't worry about being hurt. I just went in and fought. I lost. It didn't matter.

I didn't know if I'd ever fight again. Immediately after the fight, I told Cade of my nonchalant attitude toward the loss. He suggested I hang the gloves up. I didn't know if I agreed. I just knew that I conquered myself that night. I'd taken the reins of my life, if only for a night.

# 17

**April 2003:**

I never had a fear of flying until I started traveling with Joe Riggs. Mid-flight on our way to Amsterdam he leaned over to me and whispered, "Ya know, Frank, if we go down right now, BOOM, right into the ocean, this plane will be torn apart in half a second. Nobody would survive. Even if someone did survive, we're right in the middle of the damn ocean. Nobody could get here in time to rescue us...hey Frank, down we go."

Right before my departure from Brausa, Rage in the Cage matchmaker, John Petrelli, decided to take on the task of finding Joe fights that would get him some experience outside of Arizona. Joe was by far the best fighter among us, and the most marketable. He was a heavyweight. He used to weigh over three hundred pounds—and was still a heavyweight after losing nearly one hundred pounds—but he was also a knockout artist. He could box, unlike the rest of us, and he was able to send people to sleep in front of a raucous crowd thirsting for satisfaction in other people's pain.

He found a taker for Joe in Amsterdam, Holland. K-1, the largest kick boxing promotion in the world was holding a show, and wanted to mix an MMA fight onto the card to test the interest of the newer sport. I was accompanying Joe, along with John, because Roland didn't have a passport. He was born in Cuba and boated his way over to the U.S. at five years old. Roland was always worried that he couldn't obtain a passport due to his citizenship issues, and even if he could, he worried that he'd be deported upon re-entry into the U.S. For that reason, I was enlisted to act as Joe's corner man in the hedonistic city across the Atlantic.

Joe and I sat in the back of the plane in front of two college guys that let us listen to the new 50 Cent album featuring Eminem while John sat in the front of the plane alone. John was an older man, maybe late forties, early fifties during our trip, and worked full-time at Boeing as an engineer.

Joe's fight was kind of a Mixed Martial Arts fight, but in Holland, where MMA had yet to take-off, it was called a "Free Fight." The rules of the "Free Fight" match were similar to the standard MMA regulations, but had a few caveats making it part MMA, part kick boxing, with a dash of pro-wrestling sprinkled in. A person could kick box on the feet and go for takedowns and submissions while on the ground, but the fight would only be on the ground for about 30 seconds then the ref would stand the fighters up. Also, if a person was caught in a submission, he could "rope escape" by grabbing the ropes and the fight would be restarted back on the feet. Even though a fighter could escape using the ropes though, he was only allowed two escapes by grabbing the ropes. On the third, he would be disqualified. The rope escapes were the least of my worries though, on the plane, I was sitting next to Joe.

"Hey, Frank, looks like you need to take a scrub brush to that beak of yours. You got some strawberry seeds in your nose," Joe said.

The woman sitting next to him shot him a crooked eye and nosed into the conversation. "Are you two friends? That's a horrible thing to say to somebody."

"He knows it's true. And I'm a truth teller here."

"Joe, what the hell's wrong with you?" I asked, and put my head back up against the window.

As I tried to ignore the two-hundred-and-twenty-pound beast next to me the college guys behind us popped their heads over the seats.

"You know the drinking age on international flights is 18, right?"

"You hear that, Frank? Booze up, friend. Booze up."

"Oh no, I'll wait 'til after the fight. We'll booze together, friend," I said then took out two of the many Somas from my pocket I'd stocked up from my father's and threw it down my hatch, washing it down with a Coke.

"See you in Amsterdam," I said.

It was my first time flying out of the country, but for some reason it was more of an adventure about fighting in another land, than actually going to another land.

\*\*\*

John was not as impressed with the grandeur of our hotel as Joe and I. Maybe the hotel was not as fancy as we had thought, or maybe John was just used to the finer things in life? Joe and I cared less about that, and much more about the fact that we were in Europe, flown there at the expense of some other person, while we were only twenty years old. On top of all that, Joe was about to receive five thousand euros for this excursion, and I would experience the world in first-person.

Walking up to the reception desk, the cute blonde girl behind the counter asked, "You are Americans, no?" with a thick Dutch accent.

"Yes," John said. "He is fighting on the K-1 kickboxing card tomorrow night. He's one of the main events." John stood tall, his chest puffed out. He gleamed with pride as he looked at Joe.

"Oh, kickboxing is very popular here. It's a very strong sport. You get very hurt though, right?"

"Ah, ya know, we get hit, but it's not too bad," Joe stuttered.

"I think the fights are a bit violent for me, I like to watch football. What you call soccer."

After a few minutes of chitchat, we turned toward the elevator.

"What about you?" she called to me. "Do you fight too?"

"Yeah, but I'm just cornering him on this trip. I'm not fighting this weekend," I said. She smiled and we walked away.

John's room on the second floor had a large bedroom with a living room and a small kitchenette. It was a plush suite like I had only seen in movies, and didn't think I'd ever be in one—on purpose and without legal trouble, that is. Joe and I looked over the suite for a moment then found our room on the fifth floor.

"Ah hell, this has gotta be a mistake, Frank," Joe said as we opened the door to the tiny box inside. There was a queen-sized bed that took up the entire room except for a small walkway to the bathroom, a small walkway between the television, and the small fridge in the corner.

"Back down we go, friend," Joe said. "We need to take over our king's chamber and kick that old man out of our court."

I knocked on John's door. He had clearly already taken the liberty to make himself as comfortable as possible as he was wearing a bathrobe when he answered the door.

"I see you got your smoking jacket on already," Joe said.

John laughed and opened the door, but stood in the middle so we couldn't get by him to enter.

"I think they switched our rooms up. The one we just went to is tiny and only has one bed," I said.

"I don't think so. I'm pretty sure this is where they wanted me. I've built up a pretty good relationship with the promoter over the last few weeks and I think they would want me to have this room. They're going to meet us in the lobby in a couple of hours to take us to the venue. Let's meet downstairs in an hour and we'll grab lunch somewhere close before they get here for us. So, I'll see you guys down there in a bit." He shut the door.

"Well, the king has claimed his kingdom. Looks like it's back to the jester's court for us," I said.

"Dammit, Frank! Whyyyyy?" Joe yelled, holding the "y" in the air for a few seconds. "The old man won. He beat us out for the throne. Well, if we're going to live in this tiny room for a week, you're getting drunk off of these mini bottles every night."

"I am absolutely okay with that," I said.

It felt like camping. It felt like the trailer—all of us piled into one room and living and sleeping together. This time, though, there was heat, and running water, and electricity, and a mini fridge stocked with alcohol and candy bars.

\* \* \*

Nearly two years in the trailer had come to an end. When the Jehovah's Witnesses convinced my father to attend an alcohol at the Veterans Administration hospital, Chea, Adrianna, and I stayed with our older half-sister, Cathy, and her husband, John, along with their children little John, and Vinny.

We all slept in the same room, all five of us. It was warm, though, and we ate hot meals every day. Cathy cooked pasta with marinara sauce with chunks of pepperoni mixed in somewhat regularly. I thought I could have eaten nothing else for the rest of my life. We took hot baths, whether we wanted to or not, every night.

Cathy didn't care for us much. She didn't welcome us with a smile on her face, but with an annoyed sense of obligation to our father. She was the only one of his children with Annette that still talked with him. The other three hadn't spoken to him in years, but she stayed in contact. He must have had the same hypnotic spell over her as he did Chea, Adrianna, and me. I don't know if she didn't want us in her house because of the financial burden we caused her and her family—they were not well off by any standard—or if her disdain for us came from our disgusting ogre habits developed over the course of two years living in the woods. Was she upset that our father never beat us, but she and her siblings weren't so lucky? Did she hate that our father was around us all the time or that he told us he loved us regularly? I don't know, but I couldn't blame her for any negative thoughts directed at us for any of the above reasons.

We lived with her for nearly two months, packed in her little house, stuffed in the sardine can of a room, with each of our beds lined up like the little canned fish. I was happy there. Chea and Adrianna were not.

After being fatherless for the better part of sixty days, we went to visit our father at the hospital. A counselor came out to meet us, bringing us into an outside courtyard with a picnic table in the middle of the grass. She warned us that it could get very emotional, which it did. When Chea and Adrianna laid eyes on him they gushed tears. I ran up to hug him, but the whole thing felt awkward. It felt forced. I knew I was supposed to be sad for his absence and happy that we were seeing him again, so I pretended to be.

My exact feelings were unknown to me, but I felt weird. I felt uncomfortable around my family for the first time. I felt out of place with the only people I'd ever known well. My sisters and I didn't have friends. We didn't have people over to our house or go over to theirs. We had each other. There were a few classmates I'd speak with intermittently at school, but those were school friends. The only real friends I ever had were Chea and Adrianna, and being reunited with our father at the Veteran's hospital, I felt like I was looking at my family from the outside for the first time.

\* \* \*

As we sat down at the café for lunch, we looked at the television that played in the corner. An Eminem video was airing where there were naked women dancing around, but any reference to a gun or violence was bleeped out. Didn't they know they had it reversed? Joe and I both agreed we liked their way of censorship better. John didn't seem shocked by the occurrence. It could have been my indifference to guns and violence, or my enjoyment of naked women, but either way, the Dutch one-upped us there.

Our waiter finally took our order. All of us ordered some sort of sandwich and fries or chips.

"Excuse me," I said when our food arrived, "can I get some ketchup?"

He kind of nodded with an inquisitive look on his face.

"Here go," he said as he returned with a white colloidal jelly.

"Goddammit, Frank, what the hell is that?" Joe asked.

"I think its mayonnaise. I don't think we're getting ketchup here."

What could we do? We were in their country, with their shitty fry condiments. Just as I shoved the turkey sandwich into my mouth we heard a voice say, "You are Americans, yes?"

Condescendingly, Joe and I puffed up. Smiles attached themselves to both of our faces. "Yes," we said in unison.

"Oh, I feel very sorry for you. Your country is very restrictive, and this war, such nonsense. Yesterday on the news I saw someone in America got arrested for wearing a t-shirt that said he hated the president. That would never happen here."

Joe and I looked at each other as if to say, "What the hell is this nut talking about?" and Joe responded with, "You've got it all wrong, buddy."

We were somehow on the outside looking in. We were in Amsterdam for Joe's fight, but everything was backwards. We were supposed to be absorbing the culture of another country, but the culture we were scrutinizing was our own. We watched the United States through a lens just a week after President Bush ordered our troops into Iraq. We watched through reporters' cameras lenses throughout the world airing on televisions in the living rooms of countries unknown to us. We watched through the lens that the rest of the world views us through.

Petrelli assured the man and woman in their thirties that it must have been some misunderstanding. They dropped the subject after a while, but didn't seem convinced.

"Is this butter on my sandwich?" I asked while smelling the bread.

"Mayo for your fries, and butter for your sandwich," John said chuckling.

Later that night, after John embarrassed Joe and me by giving the promoter a gift basket then telling Joe he brought "Bad to the Bone" for Joe's walkout music, and after John embarrassed all of us by walking through the hotel lobby in a bathrobe to the promoter's horror, Joe and I turned on the television to witness more war coverage.

The news they showed was vivid, visceral. An amateur Russian reporter got hit in the head by shrapnel and died after an explosion. The dripping red droplets trickled down his lens as it captured its owner last words and eternal face. Then we watched, in horror, a young child, maybe four or five-years-old, get sprayed with machine gun fire as he and his family ran across an Iraqi road. His mother sprinted back to get him, carrying his dead body back with her to the others. His lifeless head dangled limp over her arm, bouncing with his mother's stride.

It was different from the outside. The news that is. It was like hearing someone else call your mother a whore or your father lazy. How could they say that? It couldn't be true, right? They don't know my parents, just like the rest of the world didn't know my America. They were just ignorant. They just didn't know what I knew.

"Jesus, this shit's depressing. Let's go for a walk," I said.

The streets were quiet. There were no humans out, just bike parts everywhere. We walked by bike tire axels. There were whole bikes chained to poles with flat tires. The cyclists during the day were everywhere, hordes of them whipped down the street in thick blob-like fashion overtaking the scenery, but now, they were gone. Everything was gone and replaced by the death of a million bikes. We were in the middle of a city that had turned into a horror story for any cycling machine. A cemetery for moving objects that were no longer moving. It was not how we pictured our first night in Amsterdam. Where were the prostitutes and smoke shops? Where were the people and the parties? Where were we, and how did we end up there? I looked at Joe, but he didn't have an answer to those questions. He was starting to wonder how he was going to win his fight against the much more seasoned opponent, Rodney Faverus. His fear was growing, and the eerie metallic cemetery was not helping him find tranquility.

We asked the blonde hotel agent when we got back what the deal was with Amsterdam. The parties? The sex? The drugs? Is everyone running around doing drugs all day? How do people live like that?

"You have been watching too much American TV," she said in her accent. "The sex for sale and drugs are legal here, but most of us don't do that at all."

"What do you mean?" I asked.

"The drugs are *legal* but not looked on in a respected manner. No Dutch person would go bragging about being in the cafes during a business meeting or anything like that. They are legal, but looked down upon. We don't care for them much here. We just tolerate them."

Joe went upstairs, and I stayed talking to her for a while. She was eventually called and had to tend to a guest.

"I will show you around Amsterdam after the fight if you want. I will show you the real Holland. I am off tomorrow from work, but I will be back here on Saturday. Would you like that?"

"Yeah. I'll see you then."

\* \* \*

It sounded like machine gun fire through the walls. Our locker room was the room directly next door to Faverus' and he started hitting mitts. The punches were loud and fast. *Could those even be real?* I thought. *Are they messing with us?*

Joe's eyes widened. His anxiety was palpable. I didn't know what to say. I said nothing. When John went to the bathroom I left on my secret mission to find the DJ and ask them if they had any Linkin Park, or something that was not "Bad to the Bone." Joe was appalled at the thought of coming out to a forty-year-old song, and ordered me to find an alternative at any point that John was out of earshot.

My mission was a success. I thought about what I would tell John I was doing when I got back into our locker room. *I'll tell him I wanted to clarify some rules.*

Just as I thought, when I opened the door John was right in front of me.

"You have to get him out of there, Santino," he said.

"Huh?"

"He's in the shower, he won't get dressed. He says he can't go out there and fight. You have to tell him something."

I walked around the corner and saw him sitting on the floor under the stream of water, naked.

"I can't go out there, Frank. I can't do it. I don't know what the hell I'm doing here."

"Joe, you have to go. We're in fucking Amsterdam. They flew us out here. You have to fight, Joe. Come on."

He sat there.

"Joe, this is fighting. This is what we want to do. Do you know how awesome this is? I would do anything to have a promoter want to fly me across the world to fight and pay me five grand. You fucking made it, Joe. Don't sit there feeling sorry for yourself when you have people like me hoping to ride your coattails to a fight half this good. Get the fuck up."

I turned the shower off. He got up.

"You're right. You're right, you're right. The goddamn sage of Phoenix, this man is, John."

"Now get dressed, creeper," I said laughing as Joe was still naked.

He laughed as I handed him his shorts and protective cup. He shut the bathroom door.

"Good, Santino. That was close," John said.

Joe was just as afraid of each fight as I'd been. He was as afraid of each fight as every other fighter has ever been. That's right, everyone's scared shitless to fight—each person just expresses it differently. Some people throw up before fights. Others slap themselves in the face and harden their exterior, so others can't see the fear. Every fighter fears the fight. Every fighter has the butterflies. Some just let the butterflies take control of them, while others teach them to fly in formation.

We warmed up and the night ticked on. There was a discomfort in the room, but nobody talked about it. We heard the crowd roar and cheer and boo from our locker room and eventually someone came to get us.

They came to get us first. We were to walk out before Faverus as we were the out-of-towners. The MC announced Joe's name and Linkin Park blared over the speakers.

"They used the wrong song," John said.

Joe gave me a "good job" look and started his walk. Above his head he held an American flag.

Loud boos filled the arena. Cups and bottles and napkins flew at us while we walked toward the ring. When we got to our corner the promoter came up to us in a fury.

"What the hell's the matter with you? Why would you bring an American flag out here like that? Put that thing away and don't take it out again!"

Faverus entered to the howls of his countrymen cheering on their homegrown American-war-mongering-slayer. He jumped over the ropes and held his arms in the air, above his head as pyrotechnics went off. He was a muscular black man with bleached blonde hair. He was a villain out of a comic book. He shouldn't have had that many muscles. It wasn't right. His jaw was huge as were his neck and arms and waist and legs.

Faverus and Joe touched gloves and the referee yelled, "Fight!"

Joe pressured him fast, backing him up with punches. Faverus circled off of the ropes and hit Joe with a good hook. Joe shot in and lifted the villain off of the ground, slamming him to the canvas. BOOM! It sounded like cannon fire as they landed. Joe wrapped up Faverus' leg in a submission hold and pulled with all his might. Faverus rolled. He rolled again. He rolled again—close enough to grab the ropes.

"Stop!" The referee pulled them apart, motioning for them both to stand.

The fighting continued.

Joe backed the brute up again. Faverus was swinging, but missing. Joe's level changes and feints were keeping Faverus off balance. Joe tripped his foe to the ground. He passed his guard—moved around his legs where he could pin him to the ground—and attacked his arm. The Dutch man flailed and made his way to his knees, then dove for the ropes.

"Stop!" The referee broke them up again.

"He's only got one more escape and Joe wins," John said to me. Both his and my eyes were peering out from below the ring in anticipation.

The fighters were back in the middle of the ring. Joe pushed Faverus into our corner. The two were only feet from John and me. Joe bent down to lift Faverus again to take him to the canvas. CRACK! Faverus' knee came up hard. Joe's head snapped back and his body lifted off of the ground. He fell face first to the canvas. He didn't move.

The ref waved the fight off and I dove into the ring. Joe stayed on the floor for another few seconds before he started to come to.

"He got me, Frank. He got me good," he said as he came to. "Damn Holland."

\* \* \*

When we got back to the hotel there was a note under the door of our room. It read:

*Dear Santino,*

*I'm sorry I missed you. I got off early, but if you'd like to meet up with me please call me.*

"Are you going to call her?" Joe asked.

"Nah, it's late."

"Well, let's call some whores. I'll get my money from Petrelli and we'll either go to a whorehouse or call them in here."

"I'm down. We should go to a hash bar too."

"Well, of course, Frank."

Joe picked up the phone and dialed John's room. He hung up a minute later.

"Old man won't give me a dime until we get back home. Says he doesn't want me to blow it here."

"Somas and the mini fridge booze?" I asked.
"You're a good man, Frank. You're a good man, indeed."

\*\*\*

Back at my father's house, after Joe and I had returned from Amsterdam, my phone rang. When I answered the raspy whisper of a salesman, or more so, a used car salesman, hit my ear. Fortunately, there was a large, physical barrier between myself, and the one of the most hated men in MMA, Shannon "The Cannon" Ritch. He was a close talker—uncomfortably close—and always grabbed onto a shoulder or an arm while leaning in to speak as if he was letting you in on a secret mission for the CIA in Mali. His dirty breath unapologetically infiltrated the barrier of decency, sneaking into unsuspecting nostrils. Even a man lacking a nose would hold his breath while engaging in conversation with him. The hatred imposed on him by the MMA community was less to do with his social mannerisms and inadequate hygienic care, and much, much more to do with his lack of heart. Not in the sense that the Tin Man was missing his heart, he had an excuse. No, Shannon would quit in a fight at the thought of danger, let alone the possibility of it. He tapped more than Bojangles or Morse Code.

Shannon's fights always started with a fury. He would throw hands and feet and every submission and strangle hold known to man with zero regard for recourse. If, when the limbs had settled, his opponent was still standing, and he almost always was, Shannon would find his way out as soon as the right moment reared its head. You don't get to 76 losses with heart. As poor a light that I've cast of Shannon while introducing him, he wasn't all that bad of a guy, and when he dropped the "Shannon the Cannon" shtick and accepted himself as merely "Shannon," he was even tolerable.

I knew of Shannon's reputation, and I assume he knew of my knowledge of said reputation, however, I was always cordial with him and even trained with him on occasion and watched a few fights at his house with him and his wife. I didn't buy into the persona that he tried to push onto others, and took him for what he was worth—a guy trying to travel the world and make some extra money for his family—but I didn't shun him either. For that reason, or whatever reasons he had, he helped me out whenever he could with booking fights or putting a good word in for me—even when it was completely unsolicited. He wasn't a bad human, just not one you'd want to emulate.

When I answered my phone I was standing in my father's living room, breathing in the clouds of smoke-filled air produced by four packs a day. All eighty cigarettes were smoked in the house daily with the windows shut. I smelled like a future emphysema patient in the making.

"Heyyyy, Santeeeno," came the long-drawn-out low whisper. "Shannon the Cannon here."

"Hi Shannon. How's it going?"

"Good. Man, have I got the opportunity of a lifetime for you. I just got off the phone with Javier Mendez. He's matchmaking for the K-1 in Las Vegas next month and they need a guy your size. I mentioned you to him and I think we can get you in."

Now, I was a decent MMA fighter, but I was the strangling type, not the punching. I was always a pretty good grappler and most of my early fights would end in somebody's limb being twisted incorrectly. In the early days of my career I could barely punch my way out of a paper bag, let alone compete at the highest level in the world at Kick Boxing. That being said, it was a paycheck and wouldn't affect my MMA record.

"Sounds good. What do I have to do?"

"Well, they know you're an MMA fighter, but do you have any kickboxing fights?"

"A few."

"Okay. I'm gonna tell him you're four and one. He won't ask questions."

"Alright. What's the pay for this and who do they want me to fight?"

"You will get eight hundred and two plane tickets to Vegas. One for you and one for your corner man, plus hotel and meal vouchers for the buffet. But, if you want to drive up, they said they will give you the flights in your purse."

"How much will that be?"

"Two hundred a person. So, you'd get twelve hundred total with the purse and the plane tickets. Not bad, huh?"

"I'm good with that, Shannon. Tell them I'll drive. Who's the opponent?"

"His name is Brian Warren. He's another MMA guy, so you should be good there. He's not a great kickboxer. Should be a good win for you. And, Santino, it's fucking K-1, bro! Do you know how big this is? This is a big fucking deal. Man, I'm always looking out for you, Santino, and I don't even want any money for this."

"Thanks, Shannon. Tell them I want it and let me know if it's a go."

I was given the fight. I went in the next day and told my trainer at the time, Trevor Lally. He was not as excited as I was.

Trevor was a small red-haired man with a goatee. He was short and small and had a twin named Todd. Both had Napoleon complexes. Trevor owned Arizona Combat Sport, the gym I started training at after my fallout with Roland and Brausa Academy. Trevor was always annoyed and cantankerous, but he was a good trainer, and his guys were always very tough.

When I told Trevor of my K-1 kickboxing match he almost choked.

"You want to fight in K-1? Seriously? I mean, you're a tough kid, but we got some work to do with you before you fight in a show like that."

"It will be fun. Anyway, I'm fighting another MMA guy. Brian Warren or something."

"Man, I always thought I'd coach someone to K-1, but I thought it would be a heavyweight. And, I'd hoped it would be for a kickboxer, not an MMA guy."

Despite Trevor's less-than-favorable reaction he agreed to train me for my short-notice fight. I trained twice a day for three weeks. I got punched more than I ever had before in my life. My head pounded. My shins ached. My hands throbbed. I ran at the Arizona State University track every other day where I combined sprints on the track with sprints up the stairs. By the end of my short-lived training camp for my K-1 debut I was as prepared as I was for my very first MMA fight.

\* \* \*

Trevor flew to Vegas, while Joe and I drove through the desolation of the desert for six hours to reach Sin City.

The fight was at the Mirage Hotel, but Joe and I stayed at a smaller hotel down the road. I wasn't a main eventer and they'd be damned if they spent the money on me for a decent room. We arrived the night before the weigh ins and walked the streets of Vegas and collected the cards of the hookers and strip clubs that the promoters slap together and hand out in the streets. We might as well have been in Amsterdam all over again. Just two kids wandering the streets wondering what it would be like to gamble in the casinos, drink at bars, bring hookers home. Any grown-up debauchery would have been fine with us, but we were young. We were poor. And more than anything, we were shy and reserved and didn't know how to be adults yet.

The next day I ate a large breakfast and lunch as I was five pounds underweight, fighting an opponent that usually fought MMA at 170-185lbs. Later that evening I faced off with my opponent, Brian Warren, after we both made weight.

"Dammit, Frank, you're a tiny little man next to him," Joe said after I got down from the stage where Warren and I squared off with fists in the air, facing one another.

"Yeah, but he's an MMA guy. A grappler too, right?"

"Damned if I know, Frank, but I do know your abs were better than his. You're a son-of-a-bitch for those abs you know? A real bastard." He was always strangely jealous of my ab muscles, and compared them to any person he saw that might rival them.

\* \* \*

I started wrestling when I was in seventh grade. I practiced Freestyle Wrestling with the team for a month or so before my first tournament, a qualifier for the Empire State Games, to be held in Buffalo NY. The qualifier was being held in Rochester, NY, and my coach, Mr. Hadsell, took me along with a few other wrestlers. I lost both of my matches, but since the top four in each division would be invited to the Empire Games, and there were only four people in my division, I technically qualified. The only caveat was that I'd have to pay the entrance fee right then and there, which I didn't have. Mr. Hadsell said it was no problem for him to pay for it and me pay him back when we got back to Geneva, the town we lived in at the time. Petrified of what my father would do if I spent $25 of his without his permission, I quickly declined the offer.

Though I didn't come close to winning my first tournament, I had fun. It was the first time I'd ever competed in my life in anything. I'd never played a sport before wrestling. I'd never even played an instrument because my father could never afford to rent the instrument from the school. Not only was I ecstatic to compete, but the entire experience was exciting. I wasn't allowed to have friends, or at least go over to friends' houses...ever. So, for me to leave for hours on a trip with other people was fantastic. It was truly the first dose of freedom I'd ever had. It was some of the first dose of reality, outside of a school setting, I'd ever had. I didn't win, but I won a bit in life, if not on the mats.

\* \* \*

## May 3, 2003:

When I got to the arena, Trevor was waiting for Joe and me. I had my hands taped professionally for the first time and hit mitts to warm up. I wasn't nervous. It didn't matter to me as it was kickboxing, and I was an MMA guy. I was going to get paid to fight a grappler in a kickboxing fight and none of it would ever affect me or my MMA career. My only issue was that the white section of my American-flag Muay Thai shorts had been dyed yellow due to me washing them with my hand wraps.

Entering the ring I was caught off guard. There were lights and cameras, a giant crowd, and sophistication that I'd never seen before in MMA. It was the largest kickboxing organization in the world and I'd immediately become of aware of that fact the moment I stepped into the ring and the lights were illuminating my pale skin. Joe and Trevor patiently waited in the corner, crouched out of sight as the bell rung for round one.

When the bell rang, I walked toward my opponent. He was large, sculpted, and ready to fight me. I saw his right shoulder and hip load up. *Right kick. He's going to throw the right kick,* I thought. CRACK! It landed flush on my thigh. It hurt like hell.

*Watch the kick again. He's going to throw it again. Pick up your leg. Check the kick.*

I didn't check the kick. SMACK! It landed flush on the exact same spot.

*Shit! That hurt a lot.* I was frozen stiff. I was a deer in headlights. Warren continued to batter my leg at will as I stood defenseless in the middle of the ring. Ding. Ding.

Finally the round was over. I hobbled back to my corner.

"My leg's fucked," I said.

"Well, it's too late now, kid. You're in there," Trevor said.

"No shit. I said that so you'd ice my leg," I said.

Joe immediately rubbed my leg with the ice bladder as Trevor instructed me to check the low kicks.

"Seconds out!" yelled the ref.

Ding. Ding.

Round two started exactly where round one left off, with my left leg getting pummeled repeatedly by a baseball bat in the arms of an angry mobster.

*Check the kick. Throw a straight right counter.* I didn't check the kick or throw the straight right counter. I was on the canvas. The leg kick dropped me. I stood up. He kicked me again. Down I went. I stood up. I hobbled around and swung a few haymaker punches at the giant beating me in front of the new, unfamiliar crowd.

CRACK! Down I went again. The fight was over. Three knockdown rule was in effect. I went down three times in one round. My first professional kickboxing fight was pathetic. I stood there and took the kicks like a punching bag.

Joe helped me out of the ring. Trevor was gone almost the second the ref counted me out. The next day I was in a wheelchair, waiting to eat at the buffet since I couldn't walk on my own. Joe saw my opponent, Brian, walking with his corner men toward us as we waited in line. He picked me up and kicked the wheelchair down the hallway before they saw me sitting.

"Don't give that bastard the satisfaction, Frank. Stand up."

# 18

When I returned from Russia, I was invigorated. My performance was awful, but it was a performance. I'd returned to Phoenix with fifteen thousand in my pocket—a large sum of money for any fighter to make at that time—especially for a fight outside of the UFC. The gym was picking up steam and we had more students than we had space. We searched for a new location. We still had time left on our lease, but since the lease was in Edwin's name, I was more than willing and happy to leave him stuck with it. I thought it proper retribution for what he did to me. Rich, the much more conscionable human, couldn't allow such a thing, so he worked out some deal with the landlord, and paid some sum of money from his own pocket so as to not have Edwin owe on the property. Even though Seth lost his IFL debut the night before I fought in Russia, Don Frye loved Seth's toughness and epic display of testicular fortitude and asked him to come back for another.

\*\*\*

Seth and I flew to Vegas to meet up with the rest of the Tucson Scorpions a few nights before the fight. The events usually had four teams competing during the night. That night, Don's Tucson team was fighting against Ken Shamrock's team from Reno, and Carlos Newton's team from Canada was competing against Renzo Gracie's New York team.

The phone in our hotel room rang early. Someone clearly forgot about the don't-call-early-on-fight-day rule and thought the sun's presence universally meant the world was awake.

"Dammit, Tino. Will you get that? Who the hell is calling this early?" Seth groaned.

"Hello," I answered.

"Hey, Santino, Don and I are going to get breakfast in about ten minutes, you want to meet us down in the lobby?" Steve Owens asked, peppy and alert.

*Old people! That's who wakes up this early,* I thought.

"Seth, you want to go eat with Don and Steve?"

"Sure."

"Yeah, we'll meet you down there in a few," I said back into the phone.

Seth popped out of his bed like a vampire from his coffin and we readied ourselves. I took more time to get ready, and was less thrilled than Seth to join the party for breakfast due to the possibility of Don being less than thrilled about my presence. He was still pretty annoyed that I signed with Bodog instead of the IFL and his team.

As the elevator door opened to the hotel lobby, I got the first glimpse of an American flag that should have been rippling in the wind high above the earth, but then I realized that it was wrapped around Don in the form of a red, white, and blue button-up dress shirt. We said our hellos and found a Mexican restaurant in the hotel lobby that served breakfast.

Steve, one of Don's assistants with the Tucson Scorpions, Seth, and I ordered coffee. Don ordered a margarita. After I ordered my food, Don turned to the waitress and said, "You might want to double check with him that he really wants that. He has a tendency of telling people he wants one thing, but then decides to do something else." He was referencing my verbal agreement to join his team, but then signing with Bodog.

Not sure how serious he was, I said, "Come on, Don, you know how the fight game is. Bodog made me a really good offer. You'd have done the same thing."

"The fight game, huh? What I know about the fight game is when a man says he's going to be joining my team, then he goes and signs with another damn fight organization," Don said.

All I could do was shrug my shoulders. Fortunately, Steve Owens chimed in, breaking the tension, asking about a mutual acquaintance of ours. Seth shot me a *well-that-was-fucking-awkward* look.

The rest of the breakfast was more entertaining after Don got his second margarita. He started on a "New cowboy singers aren't real men" rant that had us all laughing.

"How the hell are they going to be a cowboy singer without a damn hat, or boots? Hell, at least wear a real damn belt buckle!" he grumbled in his low gravelly voice. "Not even goddamn men anymore, they're pop singers."

After breakfast, Seth and I meandered around the hotel for an hour or so to pass the time and eventually retired in our hotel room until it was time to gather our things and make our way to the arena.

\* \* \*

The ring was set up in the middle of a giant meeting room. There were workers finalizing the last details on the ring, fighters bitching about not having enough water or ice in their locker rooms, coaches shadow boxing as nostalgia took over their minds and they remembered their days of glory, and so on. Seth and I decided to check out the makeshift huts in the hallway where the fighter interviews for the TV were to be held. Each hut was covered top to bottom with a respective team's gear. There were jerseys, gloves, shirts, shorts, sweatshirts, and more. Apparently, after each fight, the fighter would stand inside the hut while being interviewed in front of his teams' gear to make things look more professional.

We continued to walk around, until the fighters were directed to one of the locker rooms for the pre-fight rules meeting. As Seth and I entered, we saw Steve Owens and the rest of the team, but Don hadn't come in yet.

Piled into a small room like sardines, someone from the IFL made an announcement.

"I'm sure you have all seen the booths outside with all of the gear in it. Please don't take any of it. If you need any extra gear with your logos on it, please come to us and we will get you whatever you need. Those booths are for the TV interviews, so they have to stay looking exactly as they are."

"You might want to repeat that in Portuguese for Renzo's team," came a grumbling voice that could only be Don's. Everybody in the room snickered, and laughed. Then, a referee took the center of the room and started the rules meeting.

He went over the standard, unified, rules first: no eye gouging, no fish-hooking, no groin strikes, and all the rules that everyone knew. He then started with the IFL specific rules.

"You know there's no elbows. If you go through the ropes, and we ask you to stop, do so immediately. If you grab the ropes, you will first get a warning—" the referee was interrupted.

"Wait!" came from Don. "What's gonna happen if someone grabs the ropes?"

"Well, depending on how bad the rope grab is they may get a warning or a point deduction."

"No, goddammit. What happens if they grab the ropes with both hands?" He then motioned as if he was in a corner grabbing the ropes, one in each hand.

"Again, it depends on if it stops a takedown or not."

"Shit! What if he grabs the fucking ropes and is kicking the opponent? Stomping him in the head while he's grabbing the goddamn ropes?!" The whole time he was motioning in the air as if he had ropes in between his hands and he was stomping a grounded human.

The referee looked confused and said nothing. He just looked to the side and made eye contact with one of the IFL workers.

"Don," came from the IFL worker. "This isn't Pride. You can't kick anyone in the head on the ground at all. At any time. Ever. So no one can grab the ropes and kick anyone like that at all."

"Oh, well, that's all you had to say then, isn't it?"

The rest of the rules meeting went off without any interruptions.

Seth's fight was short, and he lost. He was heel-hooked by a fellow named Dan Molina, one of Ken Shamrock's fighters, early in the first round. Bummed about the situation, and by getting caught early in the fight, he walked up to Don, Steve, and me afterwards.

"Don't beat yourself up over it, son," Don said to Seth. "That boy didn't wanna trade punches with you. That's not real fighting anyways, rolling around on the ground like a faggot."

\* \* \*

The fighters were doing well, and the gym was making enough to cover its expenses, but I was only taking in a small income from the gym. So it was exciting that I was getting another payday in the near future. Bodog was hosting another event on August 24, 2007, and I was set to face a rather green fighter, Darren Elkins, who was 3-0, and a wrestler out of Indiana. Not only was I going to get my payday from Bodog, but I had also picked up a sponsor due to an old contact I knew from Arizona Combat Sports: MMA manager, Jason Genet. Jason got me a few thousand dollars and three 42" LCD flat screen TVs. Not only was I excited to fight, but the fear of fighting was starting to wane. The fear of getting hit and dying or having a stroke was fading. I put in a great training camp—one that I actually had time to get my cardio up and spar regularly and wrestle with my team. I was ready to fight. I needed to fight. I had bills piling up and the payday was more than going to cover them and put me on financial easy street for a few months.

As my camp wound down, I walked into the gym for my last day of sparring. It was a week out, the Saturday before the fight. I planned to spar that day, then take off Sunday and Monday, then have a few easy workouts throughout the week and focus on my weight cut the last few days. In my last rounds of the day I was on point. I slipped punches and defended takedowns and submitted my training partners. The clock read :30 during my last round. Seth was on the bottom, in his guard and I rained down a flurry of punches to finish strong. As he covered his head and tucked it toward his chest, the crown of his head was exposed through the headgear as I landed a looping punch. CRACK! The pain radiated throughout my hand and up into my arm. I knew it was broken that very second. When the bell rung, I fell to the floor and ripped my glove off. When I got the X-ray, it showed that my first metacarpal was broken all the way through. Not a string-sized piece of bone was connecting the two parts.

When I got home, Kindal's jaw dropped as I opened the door with a cast on my hand.

"What happened?" She cried out.

"I broke it."

"What are we going to do? Can you still fight? We need that money for bills!"

"Don't worry, my hand's fine. I'm okay."

I pulled out of the fight that day. Bodog never put on another show after that. They'd lost too much money in the MMA arena and cut their losses. My big contract was gone. There was nothing to do for a few months besides heal up and focus on the gym and the other fighters.

And panic about money.

The next couple of months were a financial struggle for Kindal and me. We weren't going to be evicted at any point, much to the thanks of her steady, well-paying job, but we definitely had to watch our spending. Also, we were newly married, and trying to balance our new life as financial partners and trying to figure out what our future would hold, was quite unnerving.

One Friday evening, shortly after I had gotten the cast off of my hand, Kindal and I were headed to my sister Adrianna's house to have a glass of wine and relax for a while.

"I don't feel well," she said. "I feel out of it. Almost like I'm out of my body looking in or something."

"Don't worry about it. It's stress. You've been too stressed lately. Don't worry. The gym is doing okay. I think I may be able to take some money out this month," I replied.

"I don't know. I just feel so weird."

"Trust me. I'm one hundred percent sure that it's anxiety. Once we get to Adrianna's and you get a glass of wine in you, you'll feel fine. I always feel that way when I'm close to having an anxiety attack. You're fine," I lectured.

We arrived at Adrianna's and Kindal sat down on her living room couch. Adrianna and I stood in the kitchen as I whispered, "She's super stressed. I think she's having some anxiety issues."

"I'll pour us some wine," Adrianna said.

"Thanks."

I walked into the living room. Kindal sat still as a stone gargoyle. Her face expressionless as her eyes gazed into nothingness. A moment later she let out a frightening moan; her body began lurching spastically.

"Call 911!" I yelled, as I held Kindal on the couch. Her face turned a bluish purple. Her mouth foamed. Her body continued to shake for so long. Too long. When she finally stopped seizing, she stared off again in a catatonic state. She was unresponsive. She couldn't talk.

When the police and paramedics arrived, the police asked us what drugs we were using and searched the house for some sort of contraband. We assured them again and again that no drugs were being used. Finally they stopped their interrogation and let me go to Kindal, who was being treated by the medical staff.

"Do you know who that is?" The paramedic asked Kindal, pointing to me.

She shook her head in the negative. They drove her to the hospital.

Adrianna and I got in her car to follow the ambulance and I yelled and shook and screamed as the tears streamed down my face and my voice cracked with rage and fear and every emotion I'd ever known. I was confused. I was helpless.

Hours later, Kindal began to remember things, including my name, though she couldn't pronounce it for a while. She kept saying, "Cigarrette?" But she'd shake her head, knowing that it was wrong and try again, "Sa—sa—cig—cigarrette?" Her head shook in the negative again. "Sa—sa—Santino," she finally said. Relieved, she smiled. A few days later she was released from the hospital. She had a Gran-mal seizure caused by a cavernous malformation on her frontal lobe—in layman's terms: she had an entanglement of blood vessels that bled on her brain, causing the seizure. She'd need surgery, and until completed, she'd be on anti-seizure medication.

For months I drove her to work, as her license was suspended for 90 days: a standard practice in Arizona after seizures. The hospitals are required to report any seizures to the department of motor vehicles, and, in turn, licenses are suspended temporarily. She'd take the bus or train home, as I was at the gym teaching when she got off of work.

My anxiety returned ten times worse. When I had my brain issues and surgery, it was frightening, but not catastrophic. When Kindal had her seizure, I felt mortal. I knew she was mortal. And I knew that either of us could be gone for a number of reasons any day. I didn't want to die. I didn't want her to die. I began having panic attacks after my sparring sessions. I began having nightmares of death. I was unstable again. I was scared again.

Her surgery date arrived, and she went under the knife. Dr. Spetzler, the superstar neurosurgeon at the Barrow Clinic performed a craniotomy—removing part of her skull—and then cut out a portion of her brain where the cavernous malformation was located. Once the area was gone, he replaced her skull and then she was stitched up. Upon waking up, she was in agonizing pain. She cried and shook in pain. I asked the nurse for pain medication for her.

"The doctor will be in shortly to look at her. Then she can have some pain medication."

Kindal's father, Bob, who was standing next to me as she woke up was very unsatisfied with that response. "No, you get her some damn pain meds right now!" He said, then he proceeded to berate her to where she immediately acquiesced. A moment later, Kindal's pain began to subside as the drugs began their process.

* * *

**February 2008:**

I was scheduled to fight for the IFL in Las Vegas. I definitely didn't get the grand deal that I was offered only a year earlier, though. I was offered a one-fight deal for $5,000. Losing to Rodrigo Damm in Russia didn't help me much, and the IFL was bleeding money like every other start-up MMA promotion. The real caveat, though, was that I would be fighting at 145lb, a weight that I had not fought at before but I wasn't really worried about the cut as I didn't cut a lot of weight to make 155lb at the time.

Before my IFL debut, I started working with a new boxing coach, Eric Hyer, who has also trained the likes of UFC middleweight champion, Chris Weidman. He's a coach that knows his stuff, but also a good human. Joe Riggs turned me on to him, and I began working with him almost immediately after the introduction. I also wanted to spend a few weeks in Vegas and train with Shawn Thompkins, the "coach" of my Las Vegas team, but all of my calls to him went unanswered, so I trained with my regulars at Southwest MMA.

As fight day approached, my nerves were shattering at almost every juncture. On top of my ever-frail mental state, Kindal's MMA fanatic Uncle David and her father were going to be in Vegas watching my fight—adding pressure that I really didn't want.

The night before weigh-ins, I checked my weight and saw that I was 154lb, which didn't bother me at all. I had regularly cut 8-12lb the day of weigh ins in the past, and knowing that I just had to make 146lb (145 + 1lb weight allowance for a non-title bout), the eight pounds was of no worry to me. Plus, I figured I'd lose a pound or two in my sleep. Eric was caught up in Phoenix, and was set to arrive at around noon on Thursday the day of weigh ins, so I was alone in my room that night battling my own mortality once again. I didn't want to think about my brain or Kindal's brain or either of our health anymore, so I took some Nyquil to go to bed early and get me ready for the next day.

My heart was pounding through my chest. BOOM. BOOM. BOOM. I kicked and thrashed and tossed and turned. BOOM. BOOM. BOOM. I broke out in cold sweats, then a moment later I was hot and humid and would kick the blanket off of me only to return to chattering my teeth a moment later. The Nyquil turned on me. It had happened in the past, but I'd always thought it was just Benadryl that made me jittery with anxiety and a plethora of other side-effects. I'd learn later that one of the main ingredients is the generic ingredient of Benadryl. When morning came, I felt like I'd been hit by a car after a night of drinking.

I went to check my weight. The scale read 152lb. I wasn't too worried. Six pounds wouldn't take me more than an hour to lose. It would be easy. I knew there would be some type of difference as I was going from 152lb to 146lb instead of the usual 162lb to 156lb, so I gave myself an extra hour or two to cut the weight. Weigh-ins were scheduled for 4pm, so I was going to start my weight cut around 2pm. Eric was driving up with Kindal and a few other friends of mine and would meet me at the gym where I was going to sit in the sauna.

Bored out of my mind, I began my cut just after 1pm. I covered myself in a sauna suit, which is a vinyl sweatshirt and pantsuit that traps the heat inside so your body overheats and sweats more than usual. Over the sauna suit I had on two sweatshirts and a pair of sweatpants.

I jumped on the treadmill and set the speed for 5mph. As the clock approached 30 minutes, I got off. There was moisture on my face, and I could feel drops of sweat dripping down my body inside the sauna suit, but I knew it wasn't flowing at the rate I needed it to, so I went to sit in the sauna. Matt Horwich, a fellow IFL fighter was in there attempting to make weight as well. He was reciting Bible verses out loud. I said nothing and sat on the top bench. Twenty minutes passed and I couldn't take the heat any more. I fled from the inferno and went back into the locker room and laid down on a bench. Once I felt like I could breathe again, I went back inside the sauna.

Suffocating, I wiped the sweat from my brow and ran my wet, pruned hands through my hair. The heat was drowning me. It was winning the fight. I wanted out. Once again, I ran out of the sauna to catch my breath. When I stopped sweating, I checked my weight. I knew I was close to where I had to be at, so I jumped on the scale.

*One-fifty? What the hell? There's no way! There's no way I can lose four more pounds!*

I shook my head and started texting and calling Eric. I needed him there for moral support.

"We'll be there in thirty minutes," he said. "Go back in the sauna again. Do it now. I'll be there soon and we'll keep going. Stay in there as long as you can until I get there."

I did. I went back in. He finally arrived and after hours of hell and more than one occasion of me trying to quit and just give up a percentage of my purse for not making weight I showed up to the arena for weigh-ins. I was an hour late. The entire staff was angry with me, and rightfully so, but I was there. I made weight. I squared off with my opponent, Rafael Dias, then I drank and I drank and I drank. I drank as much water and any other fluid I could get my hands on. I drank 'til I was fat and until I had the runs and sat on the toilet and then I drank more.

When Eric and I arrived at the arena the next day we began working mitts. When Shawn saw us, he commented on how amazing I looked.

"I need to go place some money on you!" He yelled enthusiastically.

When I walked to the ring I was loose. I shadow boxed on my way to the referee in charge of checking me out before I went through the ropes. I saw Kindal, her father, uncle, and my friends Brandon and Mike in the audience. When the bell rang, I was not scared of Rafael's stand up. I knew I was going to block his punches and pick him apart.

DING. DING.

We met in the center of the ring. I feinted my jab.

*Jab when he comes in. His punches are shit.*

*Here comes the overhand. Pick up your left!*

BANG! It landed on my arms. He clinched around my waist and pulled me tight into him. BAM! We hit the canvas. I didn't even put up a fight. I'm a good wrestler and I didn't put up a fight. He passed my guard. As he came around to the side of me, I worked my way to my side and tried to get back up. His arm slipped under my head and he applied a D'arce choke. I didn't defend. TAP. TAP. TAP.

I lost. I didn't care that I lost. I didn't want to be there.

I didn't want to fight.

I wanted to go home.

I didn't care about the money. I didn't care about the loss. I didn't care about the arena or looking like shit on national television.

I just plain didn't care.

I don't know if it was my anxiety of fighting due to Kindal's brain surgery or from the weight cut or if the desire to fight had finally left me. It didn't matter. I just didn't want to be there.

I went home and focused on the fighters I was training and the gym.

# 19

The world kept spinning and the guys kept winning, especially Danny Martinez and Seth. When our manager at the time told me that he had a fight for both guys in Aruba, in an all-inclusive resort, and that we'd be staying there for four days after the event, all on the promoter's dime, I couldn't buy an extra ticket for Kindal fast enough.

*  *  *

The disappearance of Natalie Holloway years ago, in Aruba, may very well be a solvable crime. Authorities may have just been looking for the wrong person the entire time. I had the experience of meeting one Aruban that most certainly should have been questioned in whatever nefarious act led to her disappearance, while cornering UFC fighter Danny Martinez on the small island. Johan Croes, Danny's opponent, a local fighter with a background in kickboxing, and an eerie stare that could make the devil himself shiver, is the man in question.

Danny had been training at my gym in Phoenix, AZ, for a few years when he got the call to fight Mark Hominick, in Montreal, on short notice. Never one to turn down a good scrap, Pancho Villa gladly accepted, and proceeded to block a record number of punches with his face—rivaling the stats of Miocic and Big Country Nelson—get dropped multiple times, and impress the hell out of the French Canadian crowd as well as the sleazy promoter, Stephane Patry.

Patry, a man that epitomizes everything Americans mock and loathe the French for, enjoyed Danny's gutsy performance, so when he decided to hold his MMA show, TKO MMA, in Aruba, Danny got the call. I suppose being a too-tough-for-your-own-good-little-gremlin-bastard does pay off sometimes. Danny was set to swap fists and bad tattoos with Johan Croes in the main event of the show in Aruba, and Seth Baczynski, another one of my fighters, also got booked on the card. The real kicker, though, is Patry flew all of the fighters and corner men to the island a few days before the event, and didn't fly us home until three days after the event, allowing us to enjoy Aruba before we returned to our miserable lives, a rarity in MMA. Usually the morning after the event you're on a plane home. With the news of the itinerary, I decided to purchase my wife a plane ticket to the paradise island to join the party. We then set off to the land of all-inclusive resorts and missing American girls.

We arrived at the resort around 10:00p.m. Seth and Danny were sharing a room and I was supposed to have my own. Unfortunately, the cheap bastard, Patry, wanted to save money and booked another corner man in the same room as me, so my wife, Kindal, and I found a room at the closest hotel we could. Fortunately, I did have my resort wristband, allowing me to indulge in all the free food and alcohol I pleased at the resort, but my wife was missing one, so I tore mine off and taped it under the protruding flap, then I paid to replace my lost band.

The days leading up to the event were exactly what we expected them to be. Kindal and I went to the beach and ate at the resort's restaurants. We played ping-pong and kayaked in the ocean. We performed the normal, standard activities that one would expect to on a vacation. The day of weigh-ins offered a minor hiccup, as Seth's opponent dropped out of the fight last minute, but Frenchy Patry assured us Seth would be paid his show money, compensating him for his time taken from work to fight, and we felt that was an adequate way to deal with the situation. Even Danny's weight cut was easy as he was fighting at 145lbs and only had to lose a couple of pounds to balance the scale.

Traveling to the venue for the fights was the first time any of us realized we were not exactly in paradise. First, unaware of the terrain and landscape of the island due to our nightly arrival, we noticed we were in the desert. We were on a desert island, not some lush tropical paradise we had expected. We expected Jamaica; we got an hour west of Phoenix. That is what you get when you don't take ten seconds out of your life to use Google. The next striking difference between our assumptions of Aruba and the real Aruba was how poor the Dutch-provincial island was. It's not Haiti, but the buildings were dilapidated and the houses weather worn and cracked. The roads outside of the tourist areas were narrow and unkempt.

The children on the side of the road weren't laughing and playing like the children in within the gates of the all-inclusive resort. They were begging on the side of the road for food and money. They were working for their families; their lives. They weren't there on vacation. They weren't there by choice.

We drove a large van on bumpy terrain for nearly thirty minutes before we pulled into a dirt parking lot. As we exited the bus there was a three-legged dog roaming the lot, begging for scraps and some back scratches. I obliged him in the latter. The building looked like an old airport hangar—an aluminum roof topped the fragile walls. Entering we found ourselves in a community center gym. It looked like a high school gym in the states, only smaller. We sat in our warmup room for the majority of the fights, but then got the itch to take a gander at the crowd and waste some time by taking in a fight or two. To our dismay, the gym was packed wall to wall with local Arubans, and they were loud. The walls of the gym rattled as the locals roared at the spectacle before them. They screamed and yelled and threw empty beer cups at fighters and corner men alike. Kindal's eyes were worried. Seth and I spoke and deemed it best that Kindal watch Danny's fight from the entranceway to our dressing room, where if she protruded her head, she could have an unobstructed view of the cage without being too conspicuous. We didn't want another blonde American girl missing in Aruba.

As Danny entered the cage, the boos were deafening. But Danny didn't care. He raised his hands high in the air and said, "Fuck 'em." Johan entered to cheers and there was no misunderstanding who the crowd wanted to win. When the bell rang Danny was quick to find his way to the center of the cage and pressure Johan. He took an unsettling leg kick early; then, according to the game plan, shot in and took the fight to the ground. He repeatedly flung and slashed his elbows at Johan's face, cutting and marking up the Aruban.

When Danny returned to the corner after the first round he was covered in another man's blood. I had to wipe his face with a towel to find the familiar features I'd known. The white towel was painted crimson. Round two began and ended, the same way the first did. Danny flung the weak wrestler to the ground and battered and beat the man with his elbows unrepentantly, and when the bell sounded he again returned covered in another's red. The fight was mercifully called off in between the second and third round. We collected our things and high-tailed our asses out of the arena and into the van.

The next day Kindal and I didn't see too much of Danny and Seth. We lounged and they drank their fill of free booze. Seth and I did, however, search for Stephane in order to get his show money. When we knocked on his room door he answered after a long five-minute wait.

"Um, 'ello?" Frenchy said.

"Hey, Stephane, we need to get Seth's show money," I said.

"Oooh, yes. Can you come back later? I am very busy right now."

"Sure. When?"

"Anytime this afternoon will work."

We returned that afternoon, but nobody answered his door. We then returned before the party being held across the street kicked off at a local bar where the TKO fighters were able to watch the UFC. Georges St. Pierre was set to rematch Matt Serra after losing his title to the New Yorker in their previous fight, and Patry, a fellow Canadian, didn't want to miss it. As the party started, Kindal and I got a table and ordered food, but before long I had to take Danny to the bathroom to begin a forty-minute vomiting session. The long hours in the sun that day combined with the free alcohol were catching up to him. On my way, I saw the slippery Patry, and yelled to Seth that he was at the bar. When I returned from the bathroom alone as Danny enjoyed his stall time, Seth informed me that Patry had heard me yell and took evasive maneuvers.

"Bastard slid away again!" I yelled.

Eventually, Danny reappeared to our table as spry as ever after he had purged the last of the alcohol he'd consumed. The situation threw another curveball when we turned to the door and saw Johan, and a crew, enter. He donned a beanie pulled low over his forehead, covering his eyebrows. He walked right up to Danny and us with a scowl on his face, then he gave him a hug and proceeded to show us all how many stitches were in his face. He looked like Jack Skellington from the Nightmare Before Christmas. Just then, Seth saw the slithering snake slide into the bathroom and we pounced like a pair of mongooses to collect his money.

"Oh, yes. Come to the room right after this and I will have your money then. I don't carry the cash with me here, you see?"

"Fine."

We left him in the bathroom and went back to the party. Danny and Seth eventually left with Johan and some of his friends. Kindal and I watched the fights. After they were over, I tried to collect Seth's show money, but to no avail. Another day passed, and I saw Patry a few more times, but he always bolted as soon as he laid an eye on me. I went to tell the news to Seth that he was probably not getting paid, but he and Danny weren't in their room.

The next day, Kindal and I went to the resort to pick up Danny and Seth to go to the airport. We knocked at the door, but nobody answered. We scoured the hotel, but they were nowhere to be found. Eventually, we had to leave for the airport without them. Sitting on the plane as the cabin door was about to shut, I feared they were lost to the currents of Aruba's riptides. Right before the door shut, though, in barged Danny, Seth, and Johan?

Johan? What the fuck?

Over way too many drinks Danny somehow got the great idea to bring an Aruban back to Phoenix like an adopted puppy. He was going to stay in

Danny's house and train at our gym. And, Danny, if I remember correctly, paid for his plane ticket, too. As I was about to close my eyes for the remainder of the flight, Johan looked over the top of his chair at me, smiled, and nodded his head. It wasn't a kind smile, though, it was a Jack Nicholson, "Honey, I'm not gonna hurt ya. I'm just gonna bash your brains in," kind of smile.

We took the wrong one home. Of all the people living in poverty in all of the third world countries, we took home one of the few humans that we should have just left alone. We didn't help a disabled kid or help a mother care for her children. No, we took home a pro fighter who sold drugs for a living.

Back in Phoenix, Johan did come to practice a time or two, but his face was rather razored up. The stitches were still very tightly holding his skin from flopping open—well that, and I think he was way more interested in partying than training. If he did come in to train, he didn't speak at all, he just shook his head and furrowed his brow and leered at everyone in the room. His haunting eyes always glaring.

# 20

Almost immediately after returning from Aruba, I'd received a call from producers for the 8th Season of *The Ultimate Fighter*. They told me that they heard I was fighting again and that I should go interview for the season. I'd already known about the upcoming season, as I'd coached one of my fighters, Efrain Escudero, on how to behave during the interview process after he got the call to go interview.

"I'm sorry. I can't do it. My wife just had brain surgery and there's no way I could leave her right now," I lied

"I'm really sorry to hear that. I hope she gets better," the producer said.

Kindal's surgery was months prior. She was doing fine. She'd be fine without me. I didn't know if I wanted to fight anymore. I had the chance to go actualize my dream of fighting in the UFC and I turned it down, again. First I turned down the Din Thomas fight, now *The Ultimate Fighter*. What the fuck was wrong with me? I had everything but a damn head on my shoulders. But, I didn't want to embarrass myself in front of the world. I didn't want to embarrass the sport. I didn't know what I wanted, but I knew I didn't want to spend six weeks in a house with a bunch of people I didn't know and have my every movement taped. That I knew.

Efrain was gone to the show, and I was, still at home tending to the gym and fighters and world of all that goes on outside of filming *The Ultimate Fighter* reality show. During this time I had a lot of soul searching to do. Did I want to fight? I didn't really know. Sometimes, I wanted nothing more than to fight. I regularly trained with UFC and WEC fighters—another MMA show owned by ZUFFA—the owners of the UFC) and on almost all occasions, I got the better of the sparring and training. On the other hand,

I never wanted to step foot in a cage again. The thought of getting in there made my palms sweat, my anxiety rise, and my sense of mortality palpable. No, I didn't know what I wanted.

But I had to find out.

I was booked to fight a journeyman fighter in North Carolina named Kevin English. He was a collegiate wrestler with a few wins, but I knew that if he beat me, regardless of the details, I didn't deserve to fight. Not that he was bad, but, I knew I was the better fighter and if I couldn't take my head out of my ass to beat a journeyman, I didn't belong in there fighting anyone. Ever.

One of my fighters, Jacob Devree, was fighting on the card with me. It was his professional debut and he easily beat his opponent by decision after three rounds. Rich Moss had flown in to corner us, and although he wasn't an MMA guru, he made me feel comfortable. Having him around me soothed me. He was a father figure, and I didn't worry when he was around. He'd always made sure everything went okay with the gym and if I ever needed anything, Rich took care of it.

"You got this, Santino," Rich said as we pummeled mitts in our dressing room. "Just don't let that mind of yours take you out of this fight. You just focus on kicking his ass and you're going to be fine."

I paced back and forth like a caged cat. I was in a zone I'd rarely been in before fights. I was close to this zone when I fought Guillard, years prior. I didn't care what Kevin English knew or how good he was at striking or submissions or wrestling. I knew I was better than him, and if I couldn't beat him I shouldn't fight again. I continued to pace. Back and forth. Shadowboxing. Scowling. Ready to fight.

I was set to walk to the cage second. As I neared the door that led to the walk-out path, I saw my opponent stepping into the cage. He looked a lot bigger than I imagined he would on fight night. His back was huge, muscular. My name was called.

"And in the red corner, fighting out of Phoenix, Arizona: Santino DeeeeFrrraaaaannnncoooooooo!"

My entrance song began: Nelly's "Number one." I waited for the chorus to begin before I started my walk, "I am number one. No matter if you like it, until you sit down and write it. I am number one. Eh—eh—eh—eh—"

I began my walk.

When the bell rang I quickly made my way to the center of the cage and stood my ground. He was a wrestler, so I was going to try to impose my stand-up on him.

*He's stiff. Watch for the shot.*

I threw a left hook, followed by a right low kick that landed on his left thigh. CRACK! The noise echoed throughout the arena. He stood on the outside, but he was too slow. I threw a jab at him, smashing it into his face and then followed it up with a low kick to the thigh again. CRACK!

*He's not checking the kicks. Keep throwing the kicks.* I did keep throwing the kicks and they landed again, and again, and again.

He clinched with me and pushed me to the cage. I circled off and landed a clean left hook to his jaw. I threw another low kick and he winced in pain. Another low kick ripped into his flesh. I could see his leg was already purple and he couldn't put almost any weight on it. I kept throwing the kicks.

I looked at the clock and saw that there was under a minute left in the round when he shot in for a takedown. I didn't remotely try to defend it. I knew I won that round, so I didn't care if I finished it on the bottom. But I thought I could throw my legs over his neck and arm and submit him with a triangle choke before the round ended, so I went to my back—a risky move.

It worked. Almost immediately I found my legs in the right place to steal his ability to maintain consciousness. He tapped almost immediately. I stood up and bowed to the crowd. They roared for me and I loved it. I felt my excitement and testosterone and fear and anger and every other emotion roll into one big ball that aroused the fight back into my veins. It felt primal. I felt like a man. A complete man.

\* \* \*

The following month I attempted to repeat the same feeling in a small show in Oklahoma, C3 Fights. Rich knew the promoter, Doctor Ron Tripp, from his days in Judo and I was matched up with an opponent that should never have been allowed in a cage. He was 1-12, and was really just another win for me. I couldn't repeat the feeling I had the month before in North Carolina, but I felt fine. Seth was scheduled to fight on the same card, but I pulled him off of it because the event was being held outdoors, and rain happened to be pouring savagely from the sky. The vinyl cage cover was a slip and slide. Seth's opponent was a formidable one, and Seth's takedown defense was still his weakness. I didn't want to risk a loss due to weird weather conditions. As for me, if I lost to a man that was 1-12, for any reason outside of a lightning strike, I knew I should just go stick my head in the sand.

The win came easy. I shot in and took Christian Nielson down and mounted him within the first thirty seconds of the bout. I cocked my elbow back to ravish his face with it, but remembered that we were on Native American land, and that we weren't required to have blood tests for HIV or hepatitis, so I changed my course of action mid-strike and settled into an armbar. He tapped almost immediately.

I was on a two-fight win streak and I felt great, granted the opponents weren't on my level, and I was supposed to beat them. But, hey, it was a start.

# 21

In December of 2008, I cornered Efrain in the finals of the eighth season of *The Ultimate Fighter*. He defeated Phillipe Nover by unanimous decision and was the first fighter out of my gym to make it to the UFC, excluding Fickett, who had reached the UFC before he came to train with us at Southwest.

After Efrain won the show, Jason Genet, the MMA manager I'd known from AZ Combat Sports, began talks with me about taking on the entire team and having a sponsor pay each member a monthly salary. Shortly after I signed with Jason, he informed me that the UFC was going to be filming another *Ultimate Fighter* season in January. Again, they would be showcasing the lightweight division. My division.

The show was, for the first time, pitting country against country. It was Team USA vs. Team United Kingdom. Michael Bisbing was the coach of the UK's team. Dan Henderson had recently won his bout against Rich Franklin to take the head spot for the USA.

I didn't want to go. I was coming back into my own with fighting and getting into a cage, but I didn't know if I was ready for that level of competition. More so, I didn't know if I wanted to be on a national TV show if I unraveled and broke down. I didn't want to be on a TV show where I was locked in a house with 15 other fighters with no communication with the outside world for six weeks: no phone calls, no radio, no TV, no books, no internet, no writing letters or receiving them from family, no leaving the house unless it was to fight or train. I didn't know if my nerves would hold up through that.

Trepidation pulled my mind and desires in the opposite direction of the show, but I did what was expected of me by—Jason and everyone else around me involved in MMA; I called the producers. I hoped that my luster had dulled and they'd ask me to attend the tryouts and maybe I'd get lost in the crowd. Seasons earlier, the UFC decided not to take videos anymore, but have applicants attend public tryouts where each hopeful contestant would have to grapple and punch mitts in a public area to get an interview. If the short interview went well at the tryouts, the fighter would be asked to fly to Vegas and be interviewed more extensively and undergo the medical testing. My hopes were dashed, and I was asked to fly to Vegas for interviews and medical testing.

*Maybe they won't accept me.* I told myself as I waited for the decision after I returned home from the process. *Who am I kidding? Everybody loves a comeback story. But maybe they have better candidates this season?*

A few days later I received a call telling me I was going to be a candidate on the 9$^{th}$ season of *The Ultimate Fighter*. I would arrive in Las Vegas in early January, and weigh-in the next day, at which point I would learn of who my opponent would be for me to fight to earn a spot in the house. If I won that fight, I was in the house and vying for a spot on the UFC roster. If I lost that fight I would be sent home immediately.

"Can't you call the WEC and see if I can get signed with them at 145lb?" I asked Jason, after learning of my invitation.

"No. They won't take you. The WEC would never poach a fighter that was invited to be on the TV show."

"Well, can I wait for the next season at 145lb? I'm small for a lightweight anyways."

"Fight on the show at 155, then drop down. Everyone does that. You have to do the show, Tino. This is your opportunity to showcase yourself to the world. This is big."

I was up against a wall. There was no way out.

Except losing that fight to get into the house.

\* \* \*

## January 2009:

I was only a few pounds over weight when I woke up in my hotel room. The weigh-ins would be in a couple of hours, and we were set to leave the gym and go directly to the UFC gym and offices, where the fights and a lot of the filming would take place.

The sauna at the gym was hot and already filled with men that I could tell just by a glance, were fighters. One fighter, Jason Pierce, was already on weight, but he wanted a safety net, so he was on a mission to cut two more pounds. *Two pounds?!* That is 32 ounces of water, which may have well been a hundred pounds or a swimming pool. Once the body has gotten near weight the pounds don't come off as easily. I've never seen anyone before or since lose more weight than needed to tip the scales favorably.

I left the sauna after the sweat began to drip from my forehead and eyebrows. I jumped on the treadmill and jogged at a slow pace—just fast enough to keep my legs from walking. Just a slow trot. I wondered who my opponent was. Would I get a chump that I'd dismantle in the first round or would they put me up against a veteran of the sport in hopes of eliminating the more seasoned guys?

We finally arrived at the UFC gym. We were standing in the gym, on the mats, when filming began. I didn't think I cared. I was there. I was going to fight. I was as calm as I could be, given the circumstances. I was about to embark on the most tumultuous six-week journey of my life, and it just didn't matter. All there was to do now was fight, and take it from there. Then, in walked Dana White, and all the calmness I'd been working toward for the last hours and days and weeks went out the window.

When Dana walks into a room, he's noticed. Not only is he a physically imposing figure, standing around 6' 1" and weighing about 250-lb, but also, he is a man of power. The latter is by far more intimidating than the former. Knowing that the bald man standing before me held my future in the palm of his hand turned me from a somewhat-confident fighter into a child waiting to be scolded by his father. As Dana lined us up, nervousness encompassed the room. People were smiling, laughing, biting their cheeks, fidgeting or, like myself, quiet as a mouse in anticipation of what was to come. Every person was more nervous than he'd ever been before.

Dana began his monologue of, "Welcome to the UFC, boys." His grin quickly disappeared as a commotion at the end of the line disrupted his train of thought. Jason Pierce was lying on the floor, his face looked plastic like a mannequin's. He had fainted.

When the commotion subsided, the fight announcements were called. I was the last fight to be announced and I squared up against Waylon Lowe, a three-time NCAA Division-II national wrestling champion. He was as wide as a house. He was a mini-pony.

The next day, we arrived at the gym early—much earlier than any of us had ever fought before. We were there at 9:00 a.m. The fights would begin promptly at 10:00 a.m. when Dana arrived. We were given a corner-man and coach to help us. I was assigned Dan Henderson's boxing coach, Gustavo, to help me get ready and to corner me.

Dana was late. The fights were delayed. The anxiety was almost visible.

At last the fights began. I'd be fighting last too.

I took long deep breaths with my eyes closed. *You can do this. You're here to win. You're going to be fine. Kindal is going to be fine. Nothing is going to happen to your brain. There is medical staff here. Win. You will win.*

I continued with the positive reinforcement again and again.

It didn't help at all.

I was scared shitless. My adrenaline had taken my legs. I was slow. I had a hard time warming up. I continued to shadow box.

"Santino, you're up next," a voice yelled through the door.

I waited outside the door in the hallway leading to the cage. When the film crew gave the go-ahead, started my walk, shadow boxing like usual and taking my time.

"No. None of that. Just get to the cage," one of the film crew said. I obliged him and jogged the rest of the way.

It was a blur from the time I arrived at the cage to when I heard the referee, Steve Mazzagotti, yell, "Fight!" There was Dana and Dan Henderson sitting cage-side. I saw Craig Pilligian and other producers sitting around the cage as well. I looked out to the gym and saw the entire roster of winners and losers watching me and Waylon.

After Mazzagotti gave the orders, Waylon and I found each other quickly in the middle of the cage. We circled. My plan was to defend the takedown and use my gargantuan reach to keep him on the outside and pick him apart. He shot in under me. I didn't defend it at all and collapsed on the canvas up against the cage. I grabbed his head and tried to bring my legs up for a triangle.

He flicked them away like a child's. He threw an elbow to my face: BANG! Another: BANG! And, yet again, another: BANG! I covered up. The elbows continued.

I didn't want to fight. I'd lost the battle against myself. I lost the will to fight.

I wanted to go home to my wife alive.

I didn't want to die in a cage on national television.

The elbows continued. I continued to cover up and offer zero offense or anything that would make the ref assume I wanted to be there. I waited for the referee to stop the fight. The elbows continued to come down on my head and neck and eyes and chest. I waited for the referee to stop the fight. I heard his corner yell. I heard people from the crowd say it was over. I waited for the referee to stop the fight.

"DING."

The round was over. Mazzogotti didn't stop the fight. *Why didn't he stop the fight?* Gustavo ran into the cage and picked me up off of the canvas and carried me back to my stool.

"What are you doing, Santino? You have to fight!" he yelled. "Do you have a family?"

"Yes."

"You need to fight for them, man. You need to fight for your family. Fight for yourself, but fight, man!"

I knew he was right. I knew Mazzagotti wasn't going to stop the fight. *My only way out of this is to fight. I have to win or I'm going to get killed in here right now. He's not stopping the fight. I have to do something.*

The bell for the second round sounded and I wearily stood and took the center of the cage. I feinted at him and he flinched. I faked a right hand and threw a left hook. He changed levels to shoot in on me. I jumped in the air and threw a flying knee.

CRACK! It landed flush on his face, but he still stood in front of me. I could tell he was wobbly and his brain had frozen.

I clinched with him and took him to the ground. He rolled away from me and tried to get back to his feet. I jumped on his back and held him with my legs. He rolled away from me to his knees. I followed. Again, he flailed. I couldn't let go. I stuck to him like a saddle to a horse. Where he went, I went. My arm wrapped around his thick horse neck. I squeezed. He tapped.

I won.

Elation warmed my body. I felt weightless as I effortlessly stood, arms raised, bright faced. Gustavo ran into the ring and hugged me.

"See, bro. You just had to fight! You had it in you!"

As I walked out of the cage, everyone stood wide-eyed and amazed by what they'd just seen. Not only did that fight not get stopped, which it very well should have, but I somehow won—in pretty spectacular fashion, too. I walked over to the table where Dana, Craig, and Dan Henderson were sitting.

"Wow. Impressive," Dana White said.

Craig smiled and gave me a thumbs up, and Dan gave me a head nod. I was much more impressed with my victory than any of them were. As I walked back to the locker room, I heard Henderson talking to Dana.

"Yeah, that was something," I heard Dan Henderson say. "That's too bad. That kid would have done good."

When I got back to the dressing rooms, I was greeted by EMT's and the doctor as a couple of the producers hovered around. I'd been elbowed repeatedly for nearly five minutes, and I was being scrutinized more carefully than the others.

"How do you feel?" the doctor asked me.

"Okay. A little foggy, but okay."

"Any nausea?"

"No."

"Headache?"

"A bit."

"Well, you did take a lot of blows, so that's pretty normal. We're going to send you to the hospital just to run some tests just to make sure everything's okay."

"Why? What do you think is wrong?"

"Nothing. We just want to be safe—given your history and all."

And into the ambulance I went.

I was on the show—something every fighter on the planet would kill for. The sheer numbers of fighters that have applied to the show, but were turned down is astounding. Even UFC champions Benson Henderson and Frankie Edgar are even among the rejected applicants. All better fighters than any of us. Much more deserving than me. Much more potential than me. But I was selected. I won my fight and gained entrance into the house. I'd waited years for this moment—years to "make it"—and, yet, I didn't want to go back. I had the golden ticket to the Chocolate Factory and I wanted to give it away.

In the hospital I sat in a private room while I waited for the CT machine to come available. I was excited at the thought of them finding something wrong with my brain. If an abnormality showed, they couldn't let me fight. Not with a brain aneurysm. But the odds were slim. I felt okay. The fear this time wasn't from my brain being injured, but my brain being normal. Healthy.

So often we forget that the cliche "be careful what you wish for" can mean so many things. It doesn't just have to mean wishing to be rich or for someone to come back from the dead or for a Monkey's Paw to give us three wishes. It doesn't have to be some ominous response to getting something for free. No, more often than not, we need to be careful for, not what we wish for, but for what we strive for. What we strive toward. Because we just might achieve it and then we have to carry through with our achievements. It's a lot harder to quit being a doctor or lawyer or CEO or professional athlete than many other professions. What happens when you dedicate your entire life to something—schooling, working, training—only to find out that when you've achieved that pinnacle, it was all for naught?

*Did I just waste my whole fucking life? What did I do all of this for? I could have spent the same amount of time I put into MMA and had three Ph.Ds or become a doctor or lawyer.*

Sitting in that hospital, I felt like my father. So often he'd tell us that he was having health issues and that he might be dying to get attention. I think deep down, he really hoped for something to be wrong. Not only would he finally be able to die, which I think he always wanted too, but he'd get the attention from his children too. He knew if he was ill, we'd be by his side. We always were. When his chest was cut open after a heart attack and doctors performed a quadruple bypass, we were by his side—waiting on him hand and foot. When he said his heart was going out on him and that the doctors told him he had months to live, we were by his side—waiting on him hand and foot. It would never change. Until, one day it did.

When I was fourteen, we'd heard all of the false wolf cries too many times. I forget what the exact ailment was this time. It sounded convoluted. It sounded so intricate that it couldn't have been real. If it were real, we'd deal with it as it arose. He was *sick...again.* He was going to *die...again.* But this time we didn't stay home. We didn't wait on him hand and foot. I went out to party with my friends—I'd started drinking and drugs and sex way too early in life—and I'd be damned if my father's lies were going to keep me in for another night of sadness. I'd lost those feelings somewhere along the way. I was immune to familial sadnesses. I barely considered him a human at that point, let alone a father. So how could I feel sadness or pity or any emotion toward an inanimate object? One that sat at the kitchen table twenty hours a day smoking cigarettes and eating pills?

So I left. My sisters had gone out as well. I didn't know where they were off to, and I didn't really care. Their life was no concern of mine. But when I came back in the morning, Adrianna was on the couch waiting for me.

"Where the hell have you been?" she shouted.

"I was at Nick's house."

"I called there. His mom said you weren't there."

"Well, I started out there, but then I went to Justin's house and—"

"Dad's in the hospital."

"Fuck. Seriously?"

"Yes, seriously!" She was becoming frantic.

"Where's Chea? What happened?"

She burst in to tears.

"He put a gun in his mouth and I had to pull it out. I had to pull it out of his mouth or he was going to shoot himself!"

"What? Why? What the hell happened?"

"I don't know. He was all fucking out of it from his meds and he was slurring his words and he got mad."

"At what?"

"Because I didn't want to sit and talk with him. For no reason. Then he started yelling that nobody wants to be around him and that he should just shoot himself since we don't want anything to do with him."

"What an asshole. Where's Chea?"

"She's at the hospital with him. They're transferring him to the VA psych ward. I don't know how long he'll be in there."

That was the first time Adrianna had to pull a gun from our father's mouth, but it wasn't the last time. He needed the attention. Me, though, I was trying to avoid it. I was trying to avoid anything except going home to Kindal and the gym. If the CT scan came back with bad news, I'd be gone. The best of both worlds: I'd have won my fight, and I wouldn't be required to stay in a house with 15 other guys for six weeks. The thought of fighting again, with my brain the way it was and under the lights—scrutinized by the world on TV—was horrific.

## 22

The CT came back clean, but the doctor did say I had a concussion. *Great! I'm going home!* The transporter wheeled me from the CT machine back to my handler from *The Ultimate Fighter*.

"So what happens now?" I asked. "Will they have to bring someone else in to take my place?"

"What do you mean?" The handler asked, a guy in his mid-twenties.

"They said I have a concussion. I can't fight with a concussion."

"The doctor said you'd be fine in a few days. It's just a concussion. You're good to go, man! You're not being sent home for that. You had a sick comeback."

And like that, I was back in.

\* \* \*

The *Ultimate Fighter* house was huge. It had to be in order to house sixteen fighters for six weeks. The show was filmed in January in North Las Vegas, just a short drive from the lights and chaos of the famous Vegas strip. Just minutes from UFC headquarters. But while most traveled to Las Vegas for the freedom of gambling and shows and drinking, we traveled to a self-imposed imprisonment. We wouldn't be able to speak with our families: no phone calls, emails, texts, or smoke signals. We couldn't walk outside the front door. We couldn't listen to the radio. There was no TV. No books. No crayons or any other hobby. Just men in a house with their clothes and training gear. But even most of the clothes and training gear was taken from us. If anything we brought had any company logos, it was pulled from our bags and stored while we were on the show. But even though we had our rules, the choice was ours to stay or not. At any point we could just walk out of that house and go home, disqualifying us from competition, and forever banning us from the big show. Others had stood in our shoes before us.

Most stayed, but more than a few were either kicked out of the house or left on their own accord—forever blacklisting them from, not only the UFC, but the entire MMA community.

I opened the front door and walked inside the house for the first time.

Outside night had fallen, but inside there was a ruckus abound. All the lights were on and the kitchen counter was covered with empty beer cans and whiskey bottles. It was nightmare come true—so many of the other seasons had been plagued by partiers drinking and pranksters playing anything but harmless jokes on each other. The worst "prank" I'd seen is from the previous season was when a group of guys jerked off on to a plate of sushi belonging to a fighter on the other team. All the sushi was consumed prior to confession. I was older than most of the other fighters; I was crankier than the other fighters, and I sure as hell didn't want anybody's semen all over my food. So when I walked into the party, I knew I was getting myself into every previous season before my own. The parties, fights, pranks, crying, and bitch fests—all on national television. *Great.*

I recognized most of the fighters from earlier in the day, the Americans, anyway. There was Mark Miller, Demarques Johsnon, Jason Pierce (the fainter), Richie Whitson, Cameron Dollar, Jason Dent, Rob Browning, Frank Lester, and Kiel Reid, and, of course, myself. *Wait. That's too many people. What's going on here?*

"What's up, man? Great comeback today," the red-headed, Richie Whitson said.

"Thanks, man."

"You get cleared and everything? Someone said you had a brain injury or something."

"Yeah, all's good."

Just then, a smaller guy came up to me, Rob Browning. He had a beer in one hand and an egg in the other hand.

"You've got a choice: You chug this beer or get the egg cracked over your head."

I laughed it off. I wasn't yet in the mood to get into a fight in the house. And although I didn't want to be there, I'd be damned if I was going to go out like that: getting into a fight in the house and getting kicked out. I wasn't that desperate.

Moments later, Rob was throwing eggs toward people playing basketball in the back yard.

"So, what's up with the extra guys? I think I counted ten of us. What's with that?" I asked Richie.

"Two guys didn't fight to get in. Kiel was supposed to fight some guy that didn't make weight, and his guy had herpes or some shit all over his face and couldn't get cleared. They brought in this guy—Junie Browning's brother (Junie Browning was the most insane human to ever grace himself on a TUF season) and another guy to fight for who gets to stay in the house.

"What's up? How've you been, man? Do you remember me?" A guy came up and asked.

"I was in the same corner as you in New Mexico last year. I fought Rashad Evan's brother."

"Oh yeah."

"Frank Lester."

"Right. How've you been?"

"Good, now that I'm here. I got to fight to stay here, though."

I roomed with Richie. I threw bags onto the bottom bunk and took a look around the house. I wandered around the house and got acquainted with both the Americans and British fighters as I took in the "Tapout" themed house—almost all of the pictures and murals and paintings were created by one of the founding members of the Tapout brand clothing company. As I wandered the hallways and introduced myself, there were the ubiquitous camera men and boom mic operators following our conversations. We were explicitly told to ignore them and to not speak directly into the camera. This was supposed to be us living in a natural environment; it was anything but. The cameramen would come and go based on what the producers living in the garage heard at any given point. See, we had necklaces on that doubled as microphones—we had to wear them any time we were awake and not training. The house was also mic'd throughout, too. Almost every corner had either a mic or camera in it. If the producers heard anything interesting, they'd send their camera goons to us immediately. Even the showers had cameras in them, and the toilets had cameras pointed directly at them—so much for privacy!

When I finally laid my head down that night to sleep, I was nervous, but proud to be where I was.

In the morning, it was all business. We were brought to the UFC gym and given our schedules. We'd be training from 8:00am to 10:00am and again from 4:00pm to 6:00pm, Monday through Friday. Saturdays were for fights. Sunday was for rest.

Each training session was set up like most training sessions I'd either been a part of, or facilitated in the past: warm up, drill, live wrestling or sparring. Rinse. Repeat.

The first few days were a bit tense as nobody knew the man standing next to him from the next, which meant we didn't know how hard to train with each other. Do I try to knock this guy out, or go light? What will he do with me? Should I try to be the toughest guy in the room, or make everyone think I'm the weakest? Strategy at its finest. I opted for not giving a fuck and just training—I think, fortunately, so did most of the other guys on the team.

My anxieties were in full force. My senses seemed heightened by the adrenaline and the constant noise of having to share a house with so many people and the lack of privacy or silence. My mind was chattering at the same rate as the others in the house. The walls started to close in on me.

As the walls closed in on me, they seemed to be closing in on Frank Lester too. He came to me the night before his fight with Kiel.

"I don't know how I'm gonna do this. I've got a baby girl at home. I'm bipolar and this house is starting to freak me out," he said.

"Don't worry about any of that stuff. Your baby girl is going to be okay. You're here for her. You're doing this for her. Remember, you have control over your mind. It's not some uncontrollable force that just runs its course. Don't listen to the negative in there. This is an opportunity, not a curse."

We continued talking for a while. Never once did I mention my own fears or insecurities.

"Thank a lot. You're my rock in here. You're gonna keep me sane in here."

*But who's going to keep me sane in here?*

Frankie, as he'd be known to us all, won his fight against Kiel and Jason Dent, and fortunately smacked Rob Browning out of the house. After the fights, Dana flipped a coin to decide which team would be given the first fight pick. The Americans got the nod and we chose Mark Miller to fight Nick Osipczak.

Our team was set, though we didn't act as one cohesive unit like the Brits. They were all one single unit, whereas Jason Dent and Jason Pierce didn't seem to want to hang out with the rest of us that much. Dent wasn't a bad guy, but being in the house bothered him maybe more than it bothered me. He was miserable in there and couldn't wait to be freed. Jason Pierce was just cranky and spent most of his time with the Brits.

Fortunately, we'd go to the gym daily and, during our commute, the drivers would turn off the cameras and let us listen to music for a few minutes.

## 23

Mark came out strong at first. He kept a quick pace and pushed the action, but Nick was so long, and deceptively crafty. Miller was a big favorite coming into that fight, but he looked slow and sluggish. Every time he'd inch forward and swing, Nick would be off to the side flicking his long limbs at Mark's head. We were all surprised to see Mark fall by way of knockout, as Nick's shin landed with a *thud!* against the back of the American's head.

We were down by one already, which doesn't really mean shit except for the fact that the Brits got to choose the next fight. The fight took place on a Saturday, so for the next few days the Americans speculated who would be the pick to fight. I was actually shocked that I hadn't been picked—my fight to get into the house was less than impressive. Initially, I thought I was on top of the world when I won comeback-of-the-year-award, but then I realized that I looked like an old sock in there getting trampled on by a mini pony.

The house was boring. We were probably the first house full of fighters that weren't drunk the whole time. We were boring ourselves. We'd tell stories of our previous lives, and I even held story time every day where both the Brits and the Americans would sit around and I'd tell a story about Drew Fickett. His tales were so absurd that they sounded like fiction, but they were true—and entertaining.

I told the listeners that I'd give them one story a day, so we didn't run out of them too soon. I got through about three weeks before they ran out. I told them of the time Drew got arrested for taking his shirt off in the airport and speaking Spanglish to the cops. I told them of the time he was caught cheating on his seven-month pregnant girlfriend, and when she barged in on him and asked if he had something to say for himself, he replied, "Why don't you go and get me and her some breakfast burritos." And I told them about the time when we were at the Abu Dhabi grappling tournament and I saw him pull a half-eaten sausage sandwich from the garbage and eat it. Eventually, though, the stories ran out and we'd go back to playing pool for five hours a day. Somehow, I came out as just as bad of a pool player as I was when I went in the house.

"Did I tell you about the time..." was the statement that become so common, we almost stopped responding to each other. We'd heard all of our stories. We'd heard all about our families and upbringings. We'd heard all about what we wanted to do when the show was done filming. We'd heard it all, and it was only the first week. My Fickett stories lasted slightly longer, but only because I rationed them. Nobody else had a rationing filter on their lives.

When the next fight announcement was to take place, we were all convinced Cameron Dollar was going to be picked, but when I walked into the gym, and saw all eyes shift toward me as our team walked past the Brits, I knew I was a marked man. Their leers burned through me like a laser. I could feel their eyes on me. In me. Infiltrating me. It was the feeling of that dream when you're in front of the class naked. They all saw right through me. I was fresh meat and they were hungry wolves, ravenous for blood. Ravenous for a win.

They picked me and Andre Winner, to be the second fight of our season. I heard they wanted to pick me first, but the producers wouldn't allow that to happen as I had a concussion and a brain aneurysm—they wanted to give me a few days to see how I was holding up.

As I walked up to stare down Andre Winner—which, by the way, how the hell do you fight a person with the last name Winner? The odds are in his favor—I saw the confidence in his eyes. He did not fear me in the least— not in the least. I didn't fear him. But I did fear myself. *Would I fight? Would I panic?* I wasn't afraid of his skills. I was afraid of my brain.

The next day, my weight cut was uneventful, and actually the easiest of my career. I only had a few pounds to lose, as I was the lightest fighter in the house. I sat in the sauna downstairs for thirty minutes and I was on weight. Occasionally, Frank and Richie would knock at the door and ask if I was okay, then I'd be left alone to the wood smell of the sauna.

When fight-day came, I woke up and went upstairs. It was early, and I couldn't sleep with the fight looming. Rarely did I ever sleep well before fights, so this was nothing out of the ordinary. What was out of the ordinary, though, was that Andre was sitting at the kitchen table. My opponent was sleeping just a mere 20 yards or so from me, which was a first—hopefully, anyway.

I've said this before, but there's something different about street fighting and a professional fight. Usually the street fights are impromptu, whereas the professional fights are set for weeks or months before the affair. But there was even something more awkward about waking up and seeing Andre sitting at the kitchen table. He wasn't a fighter or an opponent yet; it was too early in the day for that. He was just a human sitting at the table having a thought. Some people say it's a bad idea to spend time with an opponent before a fight, that it humanizes them too much. I've heard the stories of fighters going on press tours with their opponents and having to spend a lot of time together, which eventually leads to them joking and becoming somewhat of friends. Oftentimes, one of those fighters says after their loss that it was hard for them to get going in the fight, or that there was some sort of a mental block, as they'd spent time together and seemed to get along.

I wasn't going to ask Andre to join me for tea, but it was fascinating to see a person I was going to fight in an enclosed fence, sitting before me with sleep still fogging his brain, and in the corner of his eyes. I couldn't imagine sharing a roof with someone under more serious situations like a war or gladiator-style fight, where lives were on the line, but I assume others couldn't imagine being in my shoes there, while I stared at my opponent for a half of a second before he turned and recognized me.

"Funny, ain't it? Waking up and seeing each other like this, huh?" Andre said to me.

"It's definitely new. Not going to lie about that."

"Well, no hard feelings, whatever happens."

"Indeed."

\* \* \*

In the dead of night, while sleeping on the floor of the trailer, my father woke us up. My sisters and I were startled, but we didn't ask questions. We didn't know if it was a drill or real, but we couldn't take the chance. We had to move. We had to get out. Or who knows, maybe they would catch us this time?

"Go out the back window," Chea told me. She was always the leader of our unit.

My little body wriggled through the sliding window as I made my way out into the tall grass behind the trailer. Adrenaline ran through my heart. Not the exciting version. The fearful one. Chea followed me through the window. We saw Adrianna at the base of the window of the adjacent room. We met up and ran toward the woods. Our feet smacked the ground again and again at a frantic pace. We ran into the cover of the woods and met up with the foot trail toward the beaver pond. Bushes and branches whipped our arms and legs as we passed around the bend. The Native burial grounds were on our left, and I ran faster and faster by the ghosts of the non-living. My lungs burned. I could taste the iron in them. Smell it. Adrianna led our departure. Chea ensured I kept up and followed.

We made our way to the large rocks.
*Where is he?*
*He was supposed to meet us here.*
*Did they get him?*
*What will we do?*
*Where will we go?*
*Who will take care of us?*

Frantically, our brains raced. Each of us had our own thoughts of fear and panic.

The hot, wet air of summer stuck to us as a crackling came from behind some trees.

"It's okay. Let's go back inside."

Relief overtook me. We'll stay together. They won't separate me from my sisters. *Was it real? Was someone there? Did we escape their hunt or was it a drill this time?* I didn't know. I didn't care. We had to escape, and we did. Why didn't matter.

\* \* \*

I stared out the window of the van as we drove to the gym where all of the fights were held. The camera hovered close to my face, hoping to catch a quick second or two that they could use for my intro. I wondered if I was giving them what they wanted—me staring out a window. Did they want me to be animated? Talk about my wife at home? My previous shots at the show or my brain aneurysm? Maybe they wanted a mean mug? Maybe they wanted me to stare off into the distance and out toward the Vegas strip and stucco strip malls like I was doing? Maybe. As I stared at all of that stucco, I wondered if it was the last time I'd see them. Would I see the Rio Casino or the MGM Grand again? Would I see the gun stores and Chinese restaurants we passed every day to the gym again? Would I see Kindal again? Would I leave her a widow? Would she have a long life? How long would it be until she remarried? As I stared out the window, as I stared at the blurred lines of existence that whizzed by me as the van sped along, I thought about life. I thought about death. I didn't think about the fight.

\* \* \*

When the bell rang, I was calm. I moved from side to side and jabbed at Andre. He parried my punches and threw a jab of his own. I threw a kick to his mid-section. He returned in-kind with a straight right to my body. I shot in for a takedown and he circled around, shucking me off. Back to my feet I went. I swung an overhand at him—it missed by a mile. He wasn't very active. Neither was I. When he did punch, though, I could feel the bad intentions through the breeze that hit my ears and face.

*Something's got to happen. I've got to do something now.* I shot in again. Again, he sprawled, but this time I pulled him into my guard.

*Go for the triangle.* I threw my legs up toward his neck. He shrugged them off and stood up. *Thud!* His fist hist my arms.

*Thud.* He threw another. And another. And another. I covered my face and head.

"Not again. No, no, no!" I heard Gustavo yell from the corner.

Andre threw a barrage of punches at me in succession.

"Stop! Stop!" The referee yelled.

The fight was over.

I'd lost. I was out of the competition. I wasn't asked to fight on the finale. I wasn't asked to fight in the UFC on one of their "regular" cards. My career had ended. Not with a bang—well, it was actually a bang coming from a punch— not a punch to the head in devastating fashion as we stood toe-to-toe trading blows in a fight-of-the-year-battle, but to my arm as I lay in the fetal position with my hands around my head. There was nothing courageous about my loss. Nothing valiant. And there would be no second chance—or third or fourth or whatever chance at MMA that I'd actually gotten up to. The first time I spoke with *The Ultimate Fighter* producers, I made fun of Jason Thacker for his performance on the show. I'm not sure I did any better than him during my tenure in the TUF house. I'm not sure my performance was better than anyone else's in the show's history. Maybe it was. Maybe it wasn't.

I wanted to run. I wanted to escape like my father had taught us for years and years in case they came for us. In case they tried to take us away. I didn't want the cameras on me. I didn't want the embarrassment. The shame. Running wouldn't help, though. I could outrun the cameras and the fighters and the entire show, but I couldn't outrun the mirror, and eventually I'd have to look in to it. To face it.

That was the last time I stepped in the cage to fight. I'd given everything I could to MMA for my entire adult life, but it wasn't enough. It just wasn't enough to succeed. I just didn't have what it took anymore to pursue pugilism. To pursue the dream of pugilism, which I still chased. The reality of it had faded long ago.

Initially, I wanted to fight for greatness. I wanted to achieve something above myself. I wanted to climb mountains and be known for it. What I didn't want was to be known for falling off mountains. I didn't want to be known to the world as the "guy that quits" or the "guy that's great for a round, but loses any fight that goes past the first few minutes." I wanted to drift quietly into the sunset. I was okay with losing fights. If someone was a better boxer than me or wrestler or better conditioned, I could handle that. I couldn't handle giving someone a win, though. An undeserved win. I couldn't handle how I gave the win to Andre Winner. I gave it to him on a silver platter.

Would Andre have beaten me if I'd fought my hardest? Maybe. Maybe he would have. Maybe he would have knocked me out worse than any other fighter in history. But maybe not. I don't know if he would have beaten me if I'd fought him—actually fought him. But I do know that he did not beat me on that day in Las Vegas. I beat me. I gave that win to him. Maybe if I'd fought him the outcome would have been the same, but at least I'd have gone out on my shield. I didn't, though.

I crawled out of battle.

I avoided the battle.

I never wanted to run from the battle again, so I left the war. I left the army. I left the combatants to themselves to fight as they do. To fight.

But I'm also not mad about it. I'm not mad about my time in MMA. I'm not angry that I invested my entire adult life to a lost cause. I didn't fail. I'd gone my entire life wanting to be great—wanting to achieve some status where people would revere me. How fucking egotistical and megalomaniacal is that? I might not have won a world championship, but I learned that I don't need to be something I'm not. That chip on my shoulder is gone. That arrogance is gone. I learned, just as Raskolnikov learned, that he is not above others. He is not special. I am not special. I am a human just like all others. Maybe it's the failure that helped me realize these epiphanies, or maybe it's just growing older?

I don't know.

But everything I have in life, I can attribute to my life pursuing MMA. I met my wife through fighting. I started my writing career through MMA—after the *Ultimate Fighter* show aired, I began blogging for MMA websites. Later I wrote for numerous writing outlets and earned my MFA in Creative Writing. I now train fighters. Up and comers. Journeymen. World Champions. I bought a business that I run when I'm not training fighters—all possible because of MMA. I have two children that think I'm great—for the time being, that is.

I wish I could write a comeback story. I wish I could write the hero's journey where he leaves his ordinary world to find his calling and face his demons and win the girl and come home a new person to triumph in his life. And I can. I can write that story; it just has a few different paths along the way. Ones that lead to the ordinary, not the extraordinary.

And I can live with that.

# ABOUT THE AUTHOR

Santino DeFranco spent many years as a professional Mixed Martial Arts (MMA) fighter and had the opportunity to compete in front of tens of thousands of spectators as well as millions on television. He fought in such promotions as the UFC, International Fight League (IFL), Bodog Fights, Rumble on the Rock, King of the Cage, Rage in the Cage, K-1 Kickboxing and more. His fights have appeared on Fox Sports, ION television, pay-per-view and Spike TV, where he spent 12 weeks on a reality TV show, *The Ultimate Fighter.*

Santino has been published in Vice, Curious Literary Journal, Foliate Oak Literary Journal, Sherdog.com, Cagepotato.com, Mixed martialarts.com, and AZ Weekly Magazine. His memoir, *There are no Hospitals in Russia* was a finalist for the "Books for Film" contest as well. He holds an MFA in Creative Writing from Northern Arizona University.

Santino lives in Phoenix, Arizona with his wife and two children, where he trains MMA fighters and teaches English at Glendale Community College.

www.ingramcontent.com/pod-product-compliance
Lightning Source LLC
Chambersburg PA
CBHW061654040426
42446CB00010B/1740